Exploring P

Your Guide to Enchanting Cities, Mouthwatering Cuisine, and Stunning Coastal Paradises - Tips, Trips, and Plans for Every Traveler

Patricia T. Shay

PORTUGAL TOURIST MAP

Portugal

Directions

View larger map

Eucatulá Kitchen
Family-friendly

Google
Keyboard shortcuts   Map data ©2024   Terms   Report a map error

HOW TO SCAN THE QR CODE

- Open your camera app.
- Align the QR code.
- Wait for the prompt.
- Follow the link or action.
- Use a QR code scanner app if necessary

2 | EXPLORING PORTUGAL

3 | EXPLORING PORTUGAL

TABLE OF CONTENTS

Introduction 7

Overview of Portugal 7

Why Visit Portugal? 9

Best Time to Visit 12

Chapter One: Lisbon 17

Must-See Attractions 17

Best Neighborhoods to Explore 20

Dining and Nightlife 23

Day Trips from Lisbon 26

Chapter Two: Porto 30

Must-See Attractions 30

Best Neighborhoods to Explore 33

Dining and Nightlife 37

Day Trips from Porto 40

Chapter Three: The Algarve 46

Best Beaches 46

Outdoor Activities 49

Local Cuisine 53

Festivals and Events 56

Historical Sites and Palaces 60

Natural Beauty Spots 63

Local Cuisine 66

Festivals and Events 70

Chapter Four: Madeira 75

Natural Attractions 75

Hiking and Outdoor Activities 78

Local Food and Wine 82

Festivals and Events 87

Chapter Five: Accommodations 91

Hotels and Resorts 91

Budget-Friendly Options 94

Unique Stays 98

Chapter Six: Getting Around Portugal 103

Public Transportation 103

Renting a Car 107

5 | EXPLORING PORTUGAL

Biking and Walking 112

Tips for Driving in Portugal 116

Chapter Seven: Practical Information 122

Safety and Health 122

Packing Essentials 125

Local Etiquette 129

Chapter Eight: Sample Itineraries 133

3-Day Itinerary: Lisbon and Surroundings 133

7-Day Itinerary: Best of Portugal 135

10-Day Itinerary: In-Depth Exploration 139

Introduction

Overview of Portugal

Portugal, situated on the western tip of Europe on the Iberian Peninsula, is a nation recognized for its rich history, lively culture, and breathtaking natural surroundings. Its boundaries are determined by Spain to the east and the huge Atlantic Ocean to the west, giving a diversified geographical setting that includes lush vineyards, undulating plains, and golden beaches.

a. **Quick Facts**
b. **Capital:** Lisbon
c. **Population:** Approximately 10.3 million
d. **Official Language:** Portuguese
e. **Currency:** Euro (€)
f. **Time Zone:** Western European Time (WET) / Western European Summer Time (WEST)
g. **Driving Side:** Right

Highlights of Portugal

a. **Historical Richness:** Portugal is a treasure mine of historical and cultural monuments. From the old

Moorish castles to the Manueline architecture, every area of the land tells a narrative of its rich history.

b. **Breathtaking Landscapes:** The nation provides a range of stunning landscapes, from the dramatic cliffs of the Algarve to the tranquil Douro Valley, famed for its wineries and terraced slopes.

c. **Bustling Cities:** Lisbon and Porto are famed for their attractive ancient neighborhoods, bustling artistic sectors, and busy nightlife. Each city has its distinct flavor and attractions.

d. **Delicious Cuisine:** Portuguese cuisine is distinguished by excellent seafood, delectable meats, and exquisite pastries. Signature meals include bacalhau (salted fish), grilled sardines, and the famed Pastel de Nata (custard tart).

e. **Friendly Locals:** Known for their great hospitality, the Portuguese people are welcome and ready to share their culture with guests.

f. **Pleasant Climate:** With a Mediterranean climate, Portugal has mild winters and pleasant, dry summers, making it an inviting vacation year-round.

Whether you're touring ancient monuments, lounging on stunning beaches, or indulging in the local cuisine, Portugal provides a rich and fulfilling travel experience.

Why Visit Portugal?

Rich History and Culture

Portugal is rich in history, from its ancient Roman ruins to its maritime background as a seafaring country during the Age of Discoveries. Visitors may visit centuries-old castles, vast palaces, and UNESCO World Heritage sites such as the Tower of Belém and the Jerónimos Monastery in Lisbon, or the medieval heart of Porto with its distinctive Ribeira area.

Stunning Natural Landscapes

The country's various landscapes provide something for every sort of tourist. The Algarve area is famed for its beautiful beaches and majestic cliffs, suitable for sunbathing and water sports. The beautiful Douro Valley, with its terraced vineyards, is great for wine aficionados. The Azores and Madeira archipelagos have volcanic vistas, lush foliage, and distinctive flora and fauna, making them great for nature lovers and hikers.

Vibrant Cities

Lisbon and Porto, Portugal's main cities, are dynamic concentrations of culture, art, and nightlife. Lisbon's ancient areas like Alfama and Bairro Alto are packed with lovely small lanes, traditional Fado music, and lively marketplaces. Porto, famed for its port wine, provides a scenic riverbank with colorful buildings and a lively cultural environment.

Delicious Cuisine

Portuguese cuisine is recognized for its fresh ingredients and robust tastes. Seafood aficionados may enjoy delicacies like bacalhau (salted fish) served in many ways, grilled sardines, and octopus. The nation is also noted for its substantial stews, tasty sausages, and a range of cheeses. Don't miss the Pastel de Nata, a delectable custard pastry that has become a worldwide classic.

Excellent Wine

Portugal produces a broad variety of wines, from the strong reds of the Douro Valley to the crisp Vinho Verde from the Minho area. The nation is also famed for its fortified wines, such as Port and Madeira. Wine-tasting trips and vineyard visits are popular activities for wine connoisseurs.

Warm and Friendly Locals

The Portuguese are noted for their warmth and kindness. Visitors frequently comment on the warm welcome they get from people, whether in big metropolises or peaceful towns. This inviting attitude makes experiencing Portugal much more delightful.

Festivals & Events

Portugal has various festivals and events throughout the year that showcase its culture, music, and customs. The Festa de São João in Porto, the Lisbon Carnival, and the Festa de Santo António are just a few examples of exciting events where tourists may experience local traditions and enjoy music, dancing, and traditional delicacies.

Affordable Travel Destination

Compared to many Western European nations, Portugal is comparatively inexpensive. From competitively cost lodging and restaurants to public transportation and activities, tourists may have a high-quality vacation experience without breaking the bank.

Mild Climate

Portugal's Mediterranean climate offers moderate winters and bright, sunny summers, making it a perfect visit year-round. Whether you wish to escape the winter cold or enjoy a summer break by the sea, Portugal's nice weather is a key lure.

With its blend of historical richness, natural beauty, active culture, and great food, Portugal provides a unique and unforgettable travel experience that appeals to a broad variety of interests and inclinations.

Best Time to Visit

Portugal is a year-round destination with a pleasant Mediterranean climate, but the optimum time to visit depends on your interests and the experiences you desire. Here's a rundown of what each season offers:

    a. **Spring (March to May) Pros:**
- Pleasant weather with warm temperatures (15-20°C or 59-68°F)
- Blooming flowers and lush scenery, particularly in the countryside

- Fewer visitors compared to the summer months
- Ideal for outdoor activities including hiking, cycling, and sightseeing

b. **Highlights:**

- Lisbon's areas like Alfama and Bairro Alto are lively with local life.
- The Douro Valley is lovely with its terraced vineyards.
- The Algarve's beaches are less congested and great for exploring.

Summer (June to August)

a. **Pros:**

- Warm and sunny weather, suitable for beach trips (25-35°C or 77-95°F)
- Numerous festivals and events
- Lively vibe in tourist regions

b. **Cons:**

- Peak tourist season, which entails increased costs and crowded attractions
- High temperatures in certain inland places

c. **Highlights:**
- The Algarve's gorgeous beaches and pure blue seas
- Surfing at Peniche and Ericeira
- Festivals like Festa de São João in Porto and NOS Alive in

Lisbon in Autumn (September to November)

a. **Pros:**
- Mild weather (15-25°C or 59-77°F) with less crowds
- Harvest season, great for wine tours and tastings
- Beautiful fall hues in the countryside

b. **Highlights:**
- Grape harvest in the Douro Valley and Alentejo
- Mild weather for touring towns like Porto and Coimbra
- Festivals like the Wine Harvest Festival in the Douro **Valley**

Winter (December to February)

a. **Pros:**
- Mild winters compared to other European locations (8-15°C or 46-59°F)

- Fewer visitors and cheaper rates
- Festive vibe during the Christmas season

b. **Cons:**
- Cooler temperatures and increased rainfall, particularly in the north

c. **Highlights:**
- Exploring Lisbon and Porto sans the summer crowds
- Visiting the medieval cities of Sintra and Évora
- Enjoying nice nights with Portuguese comfort food and wine

Special Considerations

a. **Madeira & Azores:** These islands offer warm temperatures year-round, making them attractive getaways for any season. Spring and summer are perfect for outdoor activities and events.

b. **Algarve:** While summer is the prime season, going in the shoulder seasons (spring and fall) gives a more leisurely experience with great weather.

c. **Northern Portugal:** Regions like Porto and the Douro Valley may be wet in winter, but autumn and spring are especially attractive with temperate weather and fewer people.

Ultimately, the ideal time to visit Portugal depends on your choices. Whether you're seeking beach leisure, cultural discovery, or outdoor experiences, Portugal provides something exceptional in every season.

Chapter One: Lisbon
Must-See Attractions

Here are the must-see sights in Lisbon that you shouldn't miss:

Belém Tower (Torre de Belém):

An ancient castle built on the banks of the Tagus River is noted for its Manueline architecture and spectacular vistas. It's a UNESCO World Heritage monument and an emblem of Portugal's Age of Discoveries.

Jerónimos Monastery (Mosteiro dos Jerónimos):

Another UNESCO World Heritage property, this monastery is an example masterpiece of Manueline architecture. It holds the graves of Vasco da Gama and other famous people from Portuguese history.

São Jorge Castle (Castelo de São Jorge):

Perched on one of Lisbon's highest hills, this ancient castle provides panoramic views of the city and the river. It's a terrific spot to view historical exhibits and enjoy the gorgeous surroundings.

Alfama District:

Lisbon's oldest district is distinguished by small winding lanes, charming buildings covered with multicolored tiles (azulejos), and traditional Fado music establishments. It's a wonderful neighborhood to meander about and absorb the local ambiance.

Rossio Square (Praça do Rossio):

One of Lisbon's principal squares, historically noteworthy for its role in public meetings and festivals. It's flanked by gorgeous buildings and is a key center for shopping, eating, and people-watching.

Chiado District:

A popular quarter famed for its fine stores, theaters, and old cafés. Chiado is a cultural center where you can visit museums, and art galleries, and have a taste of Lisbon's literary and creative past.

Lisbon Oceanarium (Oceanário de Lisboa):

Located in Parque das Nações, this contemporary aquarium is one of the biggest in Europe and provides a fascinating voyage through several aquatic environments. It's a terrific family-friendly attraction with various aquatic life on show.

National Tile Museum (Museu Nacional do Azulejo):

Devoted to the art of Portuguese tiles (azulejos), this museum highlights the history, methods, and cultural relevance of these colorful ceramics. It's built in a former convent and has gorgeous tile panels and exhibitions.

Elevador de Santa Justa:

A magnificent neo-Gothic elevator that links the Baixa area to the Bairro Alto neighborhood. It boasts panoramic views of Lisbon from its terrace, making it a popular place for travelers seeking outstanding city panoramas.

Calouste Gulbenkian Museum:

Home to a large collection of art from ancient to present times, including Egyptian antiquities, European paintings, and decorative arts. The museum is nestled amid magnificent grounds, giving a calm refuge in the city.

These attractions provide a varied variety of experiences, from historical monuments and cultural places to beautiful vistas and contemporary museums, ensuring that your discovery of Lisbon is both enlightening and unforgettable.

Best Neighborhoods to Explore

Lisbon is a city with varied neighborhoods, each giving its particular beauty, history, and atmosphere. Here are some of the greatest neighborhoods to explore:

Alfama

- **Characteristics:** Lisbon's oldest district, typified by narrow cobblestone lanes, tiled buildings embellished with vivid azulejos, and traditional Fado music venues.
- **Highlights:** São Jorge Castle, Lisbon Cathedral (Sé de Lisboa), vistas like Portas do Sol and Santa Luzia, Fado Museum (Museu do Fado), and local cafés providing real Portuguese food.

Baixa

- **Characteristics:** The hub of Lisbon's city, noted for its magnificent plazas, neoclassical architecture, and lively commercial avenues.

- **Highlights:** Praça do Comércio (Commerce Square), Rossio Square (Praça do Rossio), Elevador de Santa Justa, Rua Augusta retail area, and ancient cafés including Café Nicola.

Chiado

- **Characteristics:** A stylish and bohemian quarter, noted for its beautiful boutiques, ancient theaters, and literary cafés.
- **Highlights:** Carmo Convent (Convento do Carmo), São Carlos National Theatre (Teatro Nacional de São Carlos), Bertrand Bookstore (Livraria Bertrand), Chiado Museum (Museu do Chiado), and active nightlife.

Bairro Alto

- **Characteristics:** Lisbon's nightlife neighborhood, is famed for its tiny alleyways, vibrant clubs, and unique mix of eateries.
- **Highlights:** Miradouro de São Pedro de Alcântara viewpoint, São Roque Church (Igreja de São Roque), fashionable stores and art galleries, and Fado homes giving real performances.

Belém

- **Characteristics:** A historic area situated west of Lisbon, noted for its marine history and distinctive landmarks.
- **Highlights:** Belém Tower (Torre de Belém), Jerónimos Monastery (Mosteiro dos Jerónimos), Monument to the Discoveries (Padrão dos Descobrimentos), Belém Cultural Center (Centro Cultural de Belém), and sampling the renowned Pastéis de Belém (custard tarts).

Parque das Nações

- **Characteristics:** A modern waterfront zone constructed for Expo '98, containing contemporary architecture, parks, and cultural activities.
- **Highlights:** Lisbon Oceanarium (Oceanário de Lisboa), Vasco da Gama Tower, Vasco da Gama Bridge, a cable car ride with spectacular views, and a riverbank promenade for a stroll.

Exploring these areas will offer you a thorough sense of Lisbon's rich history, lively culture, and different landscapes.

Each district has its own particular identity, making Lisbon a city that appeals to a broad variety of interests and tastes.

Dining and Nightlife

Lisbon boasts a thriving culinary scene and exciting nightlife, with a range of eating choices and entertainment places to suit every taste. Here's a guide to experiencing the finest of eating and nightlife in the city:

Dining

Traditional Portuguese Cuisine

- **Bacalhau à Brás:** A popular meal prepared with salted fish, eggs, onions, and potatoes.
- **Grilled Sardines:** Freshly caught and grilled sardines, generally eaten with salad and bread.

Pastéis de Nata: Delicious custard pastries, best served with a touch of cinnamon.

Local Favorites

- **Petiscos:** Portuguese tapas-style foods, great for sharing. Try petiscos like presunto (cured ham), queijo (cheese), and chouriço (spicy sausage).

- **Caldo Verde:** A hearty Portuguese soup prepared with kale, potatoes, and chorizo.
- **Francesinha:** A substantial sandwich from Porto, loaded with different meats and coated with melted cheese and a spicy tomato sauce.

Top Dining Areas

- **Baixa and Chiado:** Central districts with a variety of traditional and modern restaurants offering Portuguese and international cuisines.
- **Alfama:** Explore Fado establishments that blend live music performances with genuine Portuguese food.

Nightlife

Fado Houses

Experience Portugal's soulful Fado music in traditional Fado homes in Alfama and Bairro Alto. Some prominent locations are Clube de Fado and Sr. Vinho.

Bars and Rooftop Terraces

Lisbon features various rooftop bars with panoramic views of the city. Popular venues include Park Bar, Sky Bar, and Topo Chiado.

Bairro Alto

Known for its dynamic nightlife, Bairro Alto comes alive after dark with a myriad of taverns, live music venues, and tiny clubs. It's a terrific area for bar-hopping and enjoying a vibrant environment.

Lisbon's Craft Beer Scene

Explore Lisbon's developing craft beer culture with pubs and microbreweries providing a broad range of local and foreign beers. Check out Cerveteca Lisboa and Dois Corvos Cervejeira.

Lively Districts

- **Cais do Sodré:** A former red-light district turned into a hip nightlife neighborhood featuring pubs, clubs, and music venues along the coastline.
- Parque das Nações: Modern pubs and clubs situated in the Expo '98 region, giving a more modern nightlife experience.

Whether you're wanting to taste traditional Portuguese cuisine, enjoy live music, or dance the night away, Lisbon's food and nightlife scene offers something for everyone.

Explore the city's gastronomic pleasures and dynamic nightlife to fully appreciate the spirit of Lisbon's cultural diversity.

Day Trips from Lisbon

Lisbon's strategic position provides convenient day visits to adjacent cities, picturesque coastline locations, and historical attractions. Here are some fantastic day trip choices from Lisbon:

Sintra

- **Travel Time:** Approximately 30-40 minutes by rail from Lisbon.
- **Highlights:** Explore the fairy-tale village of Sintra, noted for its colorful castles, beautiful gardens, and romantic ambiance.
- **Must-See Attractions:** Pena Palace, Quinta da Regaleira, Moorish Castle (Castelo dos Mouros), and the picturesque town center with its cafés and shops.

Cascais and Estoril Coast

- **Travel Time:** About 30 minutes by rail from Lisbon.

- **Highlights:** Enjoy the coastal splendor of Cascais and Estoril, with their sandy beaches, seaside promenades, and magnificent buildings.
- **Must-See Attractions:** Cascais Marina, Boca do Inferno (Hell's Mouth), Cascais Citadel, and the Estoril Casino.

Óbidos

- **Travel Time:** Approximately 1 hour by vehicle from Lisbon.
- **Highlights:** Step back in time in the medieval village of Óbidos, encircled by ancient walls and packed with whitewashed cottages and cobblestone streets.
- **Must-See Attractions:** Óbidos Castle, stroll around the town's ramparts, visit traditional stores selling cherry liqueur (ginjinha), and enjoy panoramic views from the castle walls.

Fátima

- **Travel Time:** Around 1.5 to 2 hours by vehicle or bus from Lisbon.

- **Highlights:** Visit one of the most prominent Catholic pilgrimage destinations in the world, famed for the Sanctuary of Fátima and the Chapel of Apparitions.
- **Must-See Attractions:** Basilica of Our Lady of the Rosary, Chapel of the Apparitions, and the huge plaza where religious rituals sometimes take place.

Setúbal and the Arrábida Natural Park

- **Travel Time:** Approximately 40 minutes by vehicle from Lisbon.
- **Highlights:** Discover the natural splendor of the Arrábida Mountains and the picturesque seaside town of Setúbal, noted for its excellent seafood.
- **Must-See Attractions:** Arrábida Natural Park, Portinho da Arrábida beach, Sesimbra fishing hamlet, and the opportunity to enjoy local seafood delights.

Tomar

- **Travel Time:** About 1.5 hours by vehicle or rail from Lisbon.

- **Highlights:** Explore the ancient city of Tomar, noted for its Templar past and well-preserved medieval architecture.
- **Must-See Attractions:** Convent of Christ (Convento de Cristo), Templar Castle, and the lovely Mouchão Park.

Tips for Day Trips:

- **Transportation:** Trains and buses are excellent choices for day travel from Lisbon, providing regular services to adjacent places.
- **Timing:** Start early to make the most of your day excursion and return to Lisbon in the evening.
- **Guided Tours:** Consider attending a guided tour for a hassle-free experience and to discover more about the history and culture of each place.

These day tours from Lisbon give a superb chance to go outside the city and see the different landscapes, history, and culture of Portugal's environs.

Chapter Two: Porto

Must-See Attractions

Ribeira District

- **Description:** Porto's ancient riverbank quarter, is famed for its colorful buildings, small alleyways, and vibrant ambiance.
- **Highlights:** Explore the scenic lanes, enjoy views of the Douro River, and visit local cafés and restaurants.

Dom Luís I Bridge

- **Description:** Iconic double-deck bridge over the Douro River, constructed by Gustave Eiffel's pupil Théophile Seyrig.
- **Highlights:** Walk over the top deck for panoramic views of Porto's old center and the riverbank.

São Bento Train Station

- **Description:** Famous for its magnificent azulejo tile panels representing historical themes and Portuguese landscapes.

- **Highlights:** Admire the beautiful tile work in the great hall, portraying scenes from Portuguese history.

Clerigos Tower and Church (Torre dos Clérigos)

- **Description:** A Baroque bell tower offers stunning views of Porto's skyline from the top.
- **Highlights:** Climb the tower for panoramic views and explore the adjoining church for its magnificent interior.

Livraria Lello

- **Description:** A historic bookshop famed for its neo-Gothic building and its link with J.K. Rowling's Harry Potter series.
- **Highlights:** Explore the gorgeous interior with its unique wooden staircase and stained glass, and browse through a variety of books.

Port Wine Cellars in Vila Nova de Gaia

- **Description:** Across the Douro River, these cellars provide tastings and tours of Porto's famed port wine.

- **Highlights:** Learn about the history of port winemaking, see the vaults, and enjoy tastings with breathtaking views of Porto.

Palácio da Bolsa (Stock Exchange Palace)

- **Description:** A 19th-century neoclassical edifice notable for its lavish interiors and historical importance.
- **Highlights:** Tour the palace's great halls, notably the Arab Room with its exquisite Moorish-style ornamentation.

Foz do Douro

- **Description:** Porto's seaside neighborhood, boasts beaches, promenades, and magnificent vistas where the Douro River meets the Atlantic Ocean.
- **Highlights:** Relax on the beach, wander along the waterfront, and explore the Passeio Alegre Garden.

Museum of Serralves (Fundação de Serralves)

- **Description:** A modern art museum nestled on a magnificent parkland estate.

- **Highlights:** Explore displays of contemporary art, wander through the grounds, and explore the Art Deco Serralves Villa.

Porto Cathedral (Sé do Porto)

- **Description:** A Romanesque-style cathedral dating back to the 12th century, situated in the historic core of Porto.
- **Highlights:** Admire the cathedral's exterior and interior, and enjoy views of the city from its cloisters.

These attractions encapsulate the spirit of Porto's history, culture, and scenic beauty, providing tourists with a remarkable experience in this enchanting city.

Best Neighborhoods to Explore

Exploring Porto requires plunging into its many districts, each providing distinct experiences and an insight into the city's rich history and culture. Here are some of the nicest neighborhoods to visit in Porto:

Ribeira

- **Description:** Porto's ancient riverbank quarter, is famed for its small cobblestone alleyways, colorful houses, and vibrant ambiance.
- **Highlights:** Stroll along the riverbank promenade, enjoy views of the Dom Luís I Bridge, and visit local cafés, restaurants, and stores.

Cedofeita

- **Description:** A popular and creative area, merging traditional elegance with contemporary ingenuity.
- **Highlights:** Visit the Mercado do Bolhão (Bolhão Market), browse independent stores and art galleries, and experience the lively street art.

Baixa

- **Description:** Porto's downtown district, boasts gorgeous squares, historic buildings, and lively streets.
- **Highlights:** Explore Avenida dos Aliados, São Bento Train Station with its azulejo tiles, and the vibrant Rua de Santa Catarina retail district.

Foz do Douro

- **Description:** Porto's wealthy seaside area, where the Douro River meets the Atlantic Ocean.
- **Highlights:** Relax on the beaches, wander along the coastal promenade (Avenida do Brasil), and explore the Passeio Alegre Garden.

Bairro da Sé

- **Description:** Located around Porto Cathedral (Sé do Porto), this district is steeped in historic grandeur.
- **Highlights:** Visit Porto Cathedral, explore the small lanes packed with historic buildings, and enjoy panoramic views of the city.

Miragaia

- **Description:** A charming area overlooking the Douro River, famed for its ancient houses and attractive perspectives.
- **Highlights:** Walk along the Rua das Aldas promenade, explore the Palácio das Sereias, and enjoy views of the river from Miradouro da Vitória.

Boavista

- **Description:** A contemporary and upmarket area, with cultural organizations, commercial malls, and green spaces.
- **Highlights:** Visit Casa da Música, see the grounds of the Palácio de Cristal, and wander along the Avenida da Boavista.

Bonfim

- **Description:** A bustling area recognized for its cosmopolitan environment and traditional markets.
- **Highlights:** Explore the Mercado do Bolhão, see the Church of Santo Ildefonso with its unique blue tiles, and try real Porto food at local cafés.

Each area in Porto provides its particular character and attractions, making it a thrill to explore the city's rich cultural environment. Whether you're interested in history, art, gastronomy, or just soaking up the local environment, Porto has something to offer every tourist.

Dining and Nightlife

Porto's food scene is a fascinating combination of classic Portuguese cuisine and contemporary eating experiences. Whether you're searching for a comfortable pub for a substantial dinner or a contemporary bar for drinks, Porto provides a range of eating and nightlife alternatives to suit every taste.

Dining

Traditional Portuguese Cuisine

- **Francesinha:** A hefty sandwich with layers of cured meats, topped with melted cheese and a spicy tomato sauce.
- **Bacalhau à Gomes de Sá:** Salted codfish cooked with potatoes, onions, and eggs, a typical Portuguese cuisine.
- **Caldo Verde:** A soothing soup prepared with kale, potatoes, and chorizo meat.

Local Favorites

- **Petiscos:** Portuguese-style tapas, excellent for sharing. Try delicacies like presunto (cured ham), queijo (cheese), and chouriço (spicy sausage).
- **Pastéis de Nata:** Creamy custard tarts with a crunchy pastry shell, best savored with a dusting of cinnamon.

Top Dining Areas

- **Ribeira:** Explore riverbank eateries with views of the Douro River and traditional Portuguese food.
- **Cedofeita:** Trendy cafés and bistros presenting contemporary renditions of Portuguese food, generally with a creative twist.
- **Foz do Douro:** Upscale fish restaurants along the shore, providing fresh catches and magnificent ocean views.

Nightlife Bars and Taverns

- **Cais da Ribeira:** Historic riverbank district with pubs and taverns providing local wines, specialty beers, and traditional Portuguese spirits.

- **Galerias de Paris:** A busy nightlife zone featuring a mix of pubs, clubs, and live music venues, excellent for bar-hopping.

Wine Bars

- **Port Wine Cellars:** Located across the Douro River in Vila Nova de Gaia, where you may taste and learn about Portugal's famed port wine.
- **Prova Wine Bar:** The downtown bar offers a large range of Portuguese wines and tapas in a comfortable ambiance.

Live Music and Fado Houses

- **Fado in Porto:** Experience traditional Fado music in small places like Casa da Mariquinhas or Adega Rio Douro, noted for their authentic performances.

Rooftop Bars

- **Base Porto:** Rooftop bar offers panoramic views of Porto's skyline, serving drinks and a casual ambiance.

- **Porto Cruz Rooftop:** Rooftop terrace overlooking the Douro River, famed for its port wine cocktails and magnificent sunset views.

Late-Night Cafes

- **Moustache Coffee House:** A quiet café in Cedofeita noted for its specialty coffee and easygoing environment, suitable for late-night talks.

Porto's eating and nightlife scene reflects its dynamic culture and culinary history, providing tourists with a remarkable combination of classic tastes, innovative food, and energetic entertainment alternatives. Whether you're touring antique taverns or fashionable wine bars, Porto encourages you to taste its distinct flavors and exciting ambiance.

Day Trips from Porto

Porto's strategic position gives it a good base for seeing the different landscapes, historical attractions, and beautiful villages of northern Portugal. Here are some amazing day trip possibilities from Porto:

Douro Valley

- **Travel Time:** Approximately 1-2 hours by vehicle or rail.
- **Highlights:** Explore Portugal's famed wine area noted for its terraced vines, quintas (wine estates), and picturesque river vistas.
- **Activities:** Visit vineyards for wine tastings, enjoy a beautiful boat tour along the Douro River, and see lovely villages like Peso do Régua and Pinhão.

Guimarães

- **Travel Time:** Around 1 hour by vehicle or rail.
- **Highlights:** Known as the "birthplace of Portugal," Guimarães is a UNESCO World Heritage site with well-preserved medieval architecture and historical importance.
- **Activities:** Visit the Guimarães Castle, see the attractive historic core (Guimarães Old Town), and learn about Portuguese history in the Ducal Palace.

Braga

- **Travel Time:** Approximately 1 hour by vehicle or rail.
- **Highlights:** A historic city famed for its Baroque architecture, religious buildings, and energetic environment.
- **Activities:** Visit the Bom Jesus do Monte Sanctuary with its spectacular stairs, tour Braga Cathedral (Sé de Braga), and wander around the vibrant city center.

Aveiro

- **Travel Time:** Around 1 hour by vehicle or rail.
- **Highlights:** Dubbed the "Venice of Portugal," Aveiro is noted for its canals, colorful moliceiro boats, and Art Nouveau buildings.
- **Activities:** Take a boat excursion around the canals, see the Aveiro Cathedral, and indulge in local delicacies like ovos moles (sweet egg pastries).

Peneda-Gerês National Park

- **Travel Time:** Approximately 1.5-2 hours by automobile.

- **Highlights:** Portugal's sole national park, famed for its mountainous terrain, waterfalls, and wildlife.
- **Activities:** Hike beautiful paths, swim in natural pools, explore lovely towns like Gerês and Soajo, and appreciate the unspoiled natural beauty of the park.

Viana do Castelo

- **Travel Time:** Around 1 hour by vehicle or rail.
- **Highlights:** A picturesque coastal town famed for its historic core, traditional festivals, and closeness to excellent beaches.
- **Activities:** Visit the Santa Luzia Sanctuary for panoramic views, discover the old town with its medieval alleyways, and relax on the neighboring beaches.

Douro River Cruise

- **Travel Time:** Various choices are available, often leaving from Porto.
- **Highlights:** Enjoy a leisurely boat down the Douro River, passing through stunning vistas and vineyard-covered slopes.

- **Activities:** Choose from numerous cruise choices, including short scenic cruises or full-day trips with stops at wineries and cities along the river.

These day excursions from Porto provide a range of experiences, from experiencing ancient towns and cultural attractions to enjoying natural landscapes and wine sampling in the Douro Valley. Whether you're interested in history, wildlife, or food, northern Portugal has plenty to offer every tourist.

45 | EXPLORING PORTUGAL

Chapter Three: The Algarve
Best Beaches

When touring the Algarve, you'll discover an abundance of gorgeous beaches along its coastline, each having its particular charm and beauty. Here are some of the greatest beaches in the Algarve area of Portugal:

Praia da Marinha

- **Location:** Lagoa
- **Description:** One of the most gorgeous beaches in the Algarve, famed for its golden cliffs, brilliant blue seas, and natural arches.
- **Highlights:** Perfect for swimming, snorkeling, and exploring the caverns and rock formations around.

Praia da Falésia

- **Location:** Albufeira
- **Description:** A long length of golden beach flanked by red cliffs and pine trees, giving breathtaking views and a calm atmosphere.

Highlights: Ideal for sunbathing, wandering along the cliffs, and enjoying panoramic views of the Atlantic Ocean.

Praia de Benagil

- **Location:** Lagoa
- **Description:** Famous for its distinctive sea cave, Benagil Cave, accessible by boat or by swimming from the shore.
- **Highlights:** Explore the cave, sunbathe on the sandy beach, and enjoy boat cruises to surrounding caverns and grottoes.

Praia Dona Ana

- **Location:** Lagos
- **Description:** A tiny, secluded beach with crystal-clear waves, surrounded by stunning cliffs and rock formations.
- **Highlights:** Snorkeling, sunbathing, and enjoying the magnificent views from the cliff-top overlooks.

Praia do Camilo

- **Location:** Lagos

- **Description:** A secret treasure reached by a stairway cut into the cliffs, providing private coves and clean seas.
- **Highlights:** Swimming in the tranquil, blue waters, exploring the caverns and rock formations, and enjoying the serene ambiance.

Praia de Odeceixe

- **Location:** Odeceixe
- **Description:** Located on the boundary between the Algarve and Alentejo provinces, this beach is part of a protected natural park.
- **Highlights:** Surfing, bodyboarding, and birding along the river estuary, with a background of dunes and cliffs.

Praia da Rocha

- **Location:** Portimão
- **Description:** One of the Algarve's most popular and exciting beaches, famed for its large expanse of golden sand and dynamic ambiance.

- **Highlights:** Water sports, beach bars, and neighboring nightlife choices, making it perfect for both leisure and amusement.

Ilha de Tavira

- **Location:** Tavira
- **Description:** A cluster of sandy islands and beaches connected by boat from Tavira town, giving a natural and serene atmosphere.
- **Highlights:** Walking along desolate beaches, birding in the Ria Formosa Natural Park, and savoring delicious seafood at coastal cafés.

These beaches in the Algarve exhibit the region's natural beauty, providing something for everyone, whether you prefer calm isolation, water activities, or breathtaking coastal hikes.

Outdoor Activities

The Algarve area of Portugal is a haven for outdoor lovers, providing a broad selection of activities among its gorgeous natural landscapes and coastline vistas. Here are some wonderful outdoor activities to do in the Algarve:

Outdoor Activities in the Algarve Beach Activities

- **Swimming and Sunbathing:** Relax on the golden beaches of Praia da Marinha or Praia Dona Ana and enjoy a refreshing plunge in the crystal-clear waters.
- **Snorkeling and Diving:** Explore underwater marine life and rock formations at beaches like Praia de Benagil and Praia do Camilo.
- **Surfing and Bodyboarding:** Head to Praia da Rocha or Praia da Arrifana for outstanding surf conditions and instruction appropriate for all ability levels.

Boat Tours and Sea Excursions

- **Cave & Grotto Tours:** Take a boat tour to see the famed Benagil Cave and other sea caves around the Algarve coastline.
- **Dolphin Watching:** Join a dolphin-watching excursion from Lagos or Albufeira to view these amazing animals in their natural environment.

Hiking and Nature Walks

- **Rota Vicentina:** Explore the seaside paths of the Rota Vicentina, providing stunning vistas and unique flora and animals.
- **Monchique Mountains:** Hike through the picturesque Monchique Mountains, famed for their lush foliage, natural springs, and panoramic perspectives.

Golfing

Championship Golf Courses: Tee off at world-class golf courses such as Vilamoura, Vale do Lobo, and Quinta do Lago, surrounded by gorgeous scenery.

Cycling and Mountain Biking

- **Ecovia do Litoral:** Cycle along the Ecovia do Litoral, a coastal cycling path that spans throughout the Algarve, giving stunning vistas and easy access to beaches.

Birdwatching and Nature Reserves

- **Ria Formosa Natural Park:** Discover numerous bird species and distinct habitats in the Ria Formosa Natural Park, a refuge for birdwatchers and environment aficionados.

Water Sports

- **Kayaking and Stand-Up Paddleboarding:** Paddle along the tranquil waters of the Ria Formosa or discover sea caves and secret coves along the coast.
- **Jet Skiing and Parasailing:** Experience adrenaline-pumping water sports activities at renowned beaches including Praia da Rocha and Albufeira.

Sailing and Yachting

- **Marinas:** Rent a sailboat or yacht from Marinas in Vilamoura, Lagos, or Portimão for a day of sailing around the Algarve coastline.

These outdoor activities in the Algarve appeal to explorers, nature enthusiasts, and those seeking leisure among gorgeous natural settings. Whether you like exploring on land, sea, or beneath the water, the Algarve provides a plethora of options to enjoy its beauty and adventure.

Local Cuisine

The cuisine of the Algarve reflects its seaside surroundings, with a focus on fresh seafood, fragrant spices, and traditional Portuguese tastes. Here's a guide to sampling the great native food of the Algarve region:

Seafood & Fish Dishes

- **Grilled Sardines (Sardinhas Assadas):** Freshly caught sardines grilled and served with a splash of lemon.
- **Cataplana de Marisco:** A classic seafood stew cooked in a copper cataplana pot, comprising clams, shrimp, and fish in a rich tomato broth.
- **Arroz de Marisco:** Seafood rice cooked with a variety of shellfish, frequently seasoned with garlic, parsley, and saffron.

Shellfish Specialties

- **Percebes (Goose Barnacles):** A delicacy gathered from coastal rocks, generally cooked and served as a starter or appetizer.
- **Barnacles (Búzios):** Another kind of shellfish frequently served fresh and raw with a splash of lemon.

Meat Dishes

- **Carne de Porco à Alentejana:** Pork marinated in garlic and paprika, cooked with clams, and served with fried potatoes.
- **Feijoada:** A substantial bean stew with pig or sausage, eaten over rice and typically savored during festivals and festivities.

Traditional Snacks and Starters

- **Bolinhos de Bacalhau:** Codfish cakes prepared with mashed potatoes, codfish, and seasonings, cooked till golden and crunchy.

- **Amêijoas à Bulhão Pato:** Clams cooked in a garlic and white wine sauce, seasoned with cilantro, and served with crusty bread.

Sweets and Desserts

- **Dom Rodrigo:** A typical Algarvian treat prepared with egg yolks, sugar, almonds, and cinnamon, formed into little, multicolored cakes.
- **Figs and Almonds:** Fresh figs and almonds are widely used in sweets and pastries, such as almond cakes and fig-filled pastries.

Drinks and Beverages

- **Medronho:** A powerful fruit brandy created from the berries of the medronho tree, endemic to the Algarve area.

Portuguese Wines: Enjoy locally made wines, including crisp white wines and strong reds, typically matched with seafood meals.

Market Visits

- **Mercado Municipal de Loulé:** Explore local markets to taste fresh vegetables, seafood, and craft items, and have lunch in a typical Tasca or seafood restaurant.

Dining Experiences

- **Beira-Mar Restaurant:** Located in Albufeira, famed for its excellent seafood meals and ocean views.
- **Camilo:** In Lagos, delivering Mediterranean cuisine with a concentration on fish and local products.

Enjoying the native cuisine of the Algarve is not only about the food but also about experiencing the rich culinary traditions and tastes that distinguish this lovely area of Portugal. Whether eating in a modest pub or a beachside restaurant, each meal delivers a flavor of the Algarve's colorful culture and coastal riches.

Festivals and Events

The Algarve area of Portugal organizes a range of exciting festivals and events throughout the year, showcasing its cultural history, customs, and local delicacies. Here's a guide to some of the most important festivals and events in the Algarve:

Carnival (Carnaval)

- **Description:** Celebrated in February or March, Carnival in the Algarve comprises colorful parades, music, dancing, and spectacular costumes.
- **Highlights:** Loulé Carnival is one of the most renowned, recognized for its vivid processions and unique floats.

Festival MED

- **Description:** Held annually in June in Loulé, Festival MED honors international music and cultural diversity.
- **Highlights:** Enjoy live music performances, street cuisine, art displays, and cultural activities throughout the old city center.

Sardine Festival (Festival do Sardinha)

- **Description:** Typically held in August, this event commemorates Portugal's gastronomic legacy with grilled sardines, live music, and traditional dance.
- **Highlights:** Enjoy fresh sardines roasted over fire, accompanied by local bread and wine, in beach villages like Portimão and Olhão.

Feast of São João (Festa de São João)

- **Description:** Celebrated on June 23rd, this celebration commemorates Saint John with bonfires, fireworks, street gatherings, and traditional dance.
- **Highlights:** Join the celebrations in Albufeira, Faro, or Lagos, where residents and tourists congregate to celebrate with music, dancing, and grilled sardines.

Algarve International Piano Festival

- **Description:** Held yearly at different venues in the Algarve, showcasing classical piano music performed by famous worldwide musicians.

- **Highlights:** Attend performances at historic sites and cultural institutions, offering solo recitals, chamber music, and seminars.

Feast of Our Lady of the Sea (Festa da Nossa Senhora do Mar)

- **Description:** Celebrated in August in several coastal communities, this event commemorates the patron saint of fishermen with processions, boat blessings, and seafood feasts.
- **Highlights:** Participate in religious events, savor seafood delicacies, and see traditional marine activities.

Algarve Nature Week

- **Description:** An annual festival promoting outdoor sports and eco-tourism in the Algarve area, conducted in spring or fall.
- **Highlights:** Participate in guided hikes, birding excursions, cycling activities, and ecological workshops held around the Algarve's natural parks and reserves.

Christmas Markets and Festivities

- **Description:** During December, villages around the Algarve organize Christmas markets, including local crafts, festive decorations, and traditional delicacies.
- **Highlights:** Explore markets in locations like Faro and Tavira, enjoy seasonal music and performances, and experience Portuguese Christmas customs.

These festivals and events in the Algarve provide visitors an opportunity to immerse themselves in the region's cultural history, music, food, and natural beauty throughout the year. Whether you're experiencing local customs at Carnival or enjoying live music at Festival MED, each event highlights the Algarve's dynamic energy and community festivals.

Sintra

Historical Sites and Palaces

Sintra is home to numerous spectacular historical landmarks and palaces, each looking into Portugal's rich cultural and architectural past. Here are some of the must-visit historical buildings and palaces in Sintra:

Historical Sites & Palaces in Sintra Pena Palace (Palácio da Pena)

- **Description:** A Romanticist castle notable for its brilliant colors, beautiful brickwork, and combination of architectural styles.

- **Highlights:** Explore the palace's magnificent interiors, including the remarkable Dom Fernando II's private apartments, and enjoy panoramic views from its hilltop elevation.

Quinta da Regaleira

- **Description:** A UNESCO World Heritage site includes a Gothic castle, magnificent gardens, and a network of tunnels and caverns.

- **Highlights:** Visit the initiation well (Poço Iniciático), and spiral staircase, and explore the magnificent grounds filled with lakes, fountains, and significant buildings.

Sintra National Palace (Palácio Nacional de Sintra)

- **Description:** Located in the center of Sintra's old town, this palace is recognized for its characteristic twin chimneys and Mudejar (Moorish) architecture.
- **Highlights:** Tour the royal rooms, notably the Sala dos Cisnes (Swan Room) and Sala dos Brasões (Coat of Arms Room), embellished with elaborate tilework.

Castle of the Moors (Castelo dos Mouros)

- **Description:** A medieval fortress set on a mountaintop overlooking Sintra, erected during the 8th and 9th centuries by the Moors.
- **Highlights:** Walk around the ramparts for spectacular views of Sintra and its surrounds, and study the archeological remnants and defensive walls.

Monserrate Palace (Palácio de Monserrate)

- **Description:** A Romanticist palace surrounded by botanical gardens, with a combination of Gothic, Indian, and Moorish architectural influences.

- **Highlights:** Wander around the magnificent gardens with exotic plant species, water features, and the gorgeous castle with its elaborate detailing.

Convent of the Capuchos (Convento dos Capuchos)

- **Description:** A quiet Franciscan monastery going back to the 16th century, notable for its simple stone cells and natural absorption into the surrounding terrain.
- **Highlights:** Explore the monastery's short hallways, chapels, and tiny monk cells, experiencing the simplicity and quiet of the Franciscan way of life.

These historical ruins and palaces in Sintra provide a fascinating trip through numerous architectural styles, cultural influences, and natural beauty, making Sintra a genuinely wonderful destination for travelers discovering Portugal's legacy.

Natural Beauty Spots

Sintra's natural beauty is as appealing as its medieval palaces and architectural marvels. Here are some of the most stunning natural sites to visit in and around Sintra:

Natural Beauty Spots in Sintra Pena Park (Parque da Pena)

- **Description:** Surrounding Pena Palace, this park is a beautiful wooded region with meandering trails, secret gardens, and breathtaking overlooks.
- **Highlights:** Discover the Queen's Fern Valley, and the Chalet of the Countess of Edla, and enjoy panoramic views from the Cruz Alta overlook.

Monserrate Park (Parque de Monserrate)

- **Description:** Adjacent to Monserrate Palace, this park has exotic gardens with flora from all over the globe, following the Romanticist style.
- **Highlights:** Explore the Waterfall Valley, the Mexican Garden, and the Rose Garden, recognized for their botanical richness and scenic splendor.

Peninha Sanctuary (Santuário do Peninha)

- **Description:** Located atop the Sintra Mountains, affording magnificent views of the Atlantic Ocean and surrounding landscape.

- Highlights: Visit the church of Nossa Senhora da Peninha, explore trekking routes through mountainous terrain, and see spectacular sunset views.

Cabo da Roca

- **Description:** The westernmost point of continental Europe, famed for its stunning cliffs and Atlantic Ocean vistas.

Highlights: Visit the landmark Cabo da Roca lighthouse, explore coastal paths along the cliffs, and take in the raw beauty of the coastline.

Adraga Beach (Praia da Adraga)

- **Description:** A gorgeous beach hidden between cliffs, offering golden beaches, clean seas, and natural rock formations.
- **Highlights:** Relax on the beach, discover tidal pools, and observe the stunning beauty of the craggy coastline.

Pedra Amarela Belvedere (Miradouro da Pedra Amarela)

- **Description:** A lesser-known overlook affording sweeping views of Sintra's trees and shoreline.
- **Highlights:** Enjoy a tranquil setting, great for picnics, photography, and soaking in the serene splendor of the Sintra scenery.

These natural beauty sites in Sintra give chances for hiking, photography, relaxing, and experiencing the region's unique flora and fauna. Whether you're enjoying panoramic views from hilltop parks or exploring quiet beaches and cliffs, Sintra's natural beauty provides amazing experiences for tourists.

Local Cuisine

Sintra provides a delicious selection of local food that reflects both its seaside surroundings and the ancient culinary traditions of Portugal. Here are some foods and delicacies to sample while discovering the culinary joys of Sintra:

Queijadas de Sintra

- **Description:** Traditional Portuguese pastries are prepared with a sweet, delicate crust with a filling of creamy cheese, eggs, and sugar.
- **Where to Find:** Look for them at local bakeries and pastry shops across Sintra.

Travesseiros

- **Description:** Flaky puff pastry filled with almond cream and coated with powdered sugar, coming from the legendary Piriquita bakery.
- **Where to Find:** Piriquita is a renowned bakery in Sintra noted for its unique Travesseiros.

Sardinhas Assadas

- **Description:** Grilled sardines, a mainstay of Portuguese cuisine, seasoned with sea salt and served with a drizzle of olive oil and a slice of lemon.
- **Where to Find:** Look for them at traditional seafood restaurants and tasquinhas (taverns) in Sintra.

Caldo Verde

- **Description:** A substantial soup prepared with potatoes, collard greens, chorizo or Portuguese sausage, and olive oil.
- **Where to Find:** Enjoy this warm soup at local cafés and restaurants in Sintra.

Arroz de Marisco

- **Description:** A savory seafood rice meal cooked with a variety of shellfish such as clams, shrimp, and occasionally crab, seasoned with garlic, tomatoes, and fresh herbs.
- **Where to Find:** Look for it at seafood restaurants and tasquinhas around Sintra.

Bacalhau à Brás

- **Description:** Shredded salted fish combined with onions, finely sliced potatoes, and scrambled eggs, seasoned with parsley and olives.
- **Where to Find:** Available at traditional Portuguese restaurants in Sintra, generally served as a main dish.

Pastéis de Nata

- **Description:** Portugal's famed custard tarts with a crispy pastry crust and a creamy custard interior, frequently coated with cinnamon or powdered sugar.
- **Where to Find:** Enjoy them in local cafés and bakeries in Sintra, excellent for a sweet treat with coffee or tea.

Ginjinha

- **Description:** A classic Portuguese liqueur prepared from sour cherries (ginjas), often served in a chocolate cup or as a shot.
- **Where to Find:** Look for Ginjinha at pubs and taverns in Sintra, commonly served as a digestif after a meal.

These local meals and delicacies provide a sense of Sintra's gastronomic history, merging classic Portuguese tastes with regional influences. Whether you're seeing ancient monuments or enjoying the natural beauty of Sintra, consuming its native food adds a wonderful layer to your stay.

Festivals and Events

Sintra, with its rich cultural past and scenic surroundings, holds various festivals and events throughout the year that commemorate its history, arts, and local customs. Here are some of the important festivals and events in Sintra:

Festivals & Events in Sintra Sintra Music Festival

- **Description:** An annual music event conducted in different historic sites and gardens across Sintra.
- **Highlights:** Enjoy classical music performances by famous performers, chamber music concerts, and recitals in evocative settings.

Feira Saloia de Belas

- **Description:** A traditional fair honoring the agricultural and cultural traditions of the Sintra area.
- **Highlights:** Experience folk music and dance performances, local crafts and artisanal items, traditional cuisine and wine tastings, and cultural displays.

Sintra Dance Festival

- **Description:** A dance festival including performances by local and international dance organizations, displaying a range of dance styles including ballet, contemporary dance, and traditional Portuguese dance.
- **Highlights:** Attend dancing workshops, masterclasses, and outdoor performances in gorgeous settings around Sintra.

Sintra Food Festival

- **Description:** A gastronomic festival showcasing local gastronomy and traditional Portuguese cuisine.
- **Highlights:** Sample regional delicacies and specialties from Sintra and the surrounding regions, participate in culinary demos and food tastings, and enjoy live music and entertainment.

Feira Medieval de Sintra

- **Description:** A medieval fair conducted yearly in the historic core of Sintra, converting the town into a medieval hamlet.

- **Highlights:** Experience reenactments, jousting contests, medieval music and dance performances, artisan workshops, and authentic medieval food.

Christmas and New Year Celebrations

- **Description:** Festive activities and festivities over the holiday season, including Christmas markets, concerts, nativity scenes, and New Year's Eve fireworks.
- **Highlights:** Visit Sintra's adorned streets and ancient squares, consume seasonal snacks and traditional sweets, and join in festive celebrations.

Cultural Events and Exhibitions

- **Description:** Throughout the year, Sintra presents different cultural events, art exhibits, and theatrical performances in its ancient palaces, museums, and galleries.
- **Highlights:** Attend art exhibits showcasing local and international artists, cultural seminars and lectures, and theatrical performances in unique and evocative settings.

These festivals and events in Sintra provide visitors with a unique chance to immerse themselves in the region's cultural history, arts, music, and gastronomic traditions throughout the year. Whether you're touring ancient buildings or enjoying the natural beauty of Sintra's surroundings, attending a local festival adds a vivid and festive dimension to your stay.

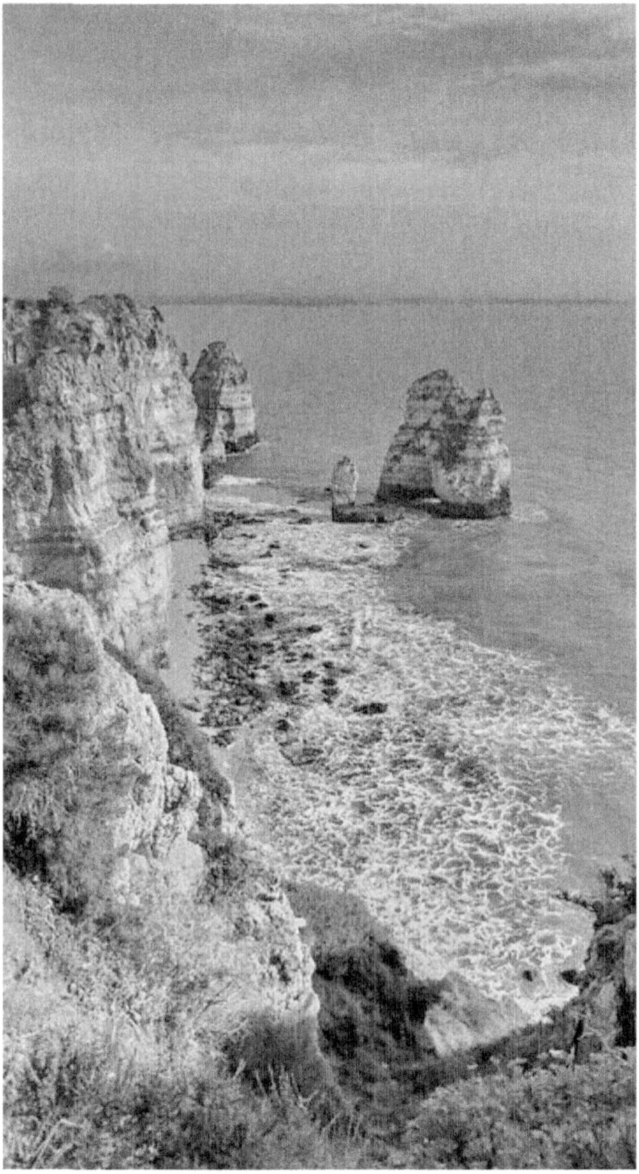

Chapter Four: Madeira

Natural Attractions

Madeira is recognized for its magnificent natural beauty, typified by lush landscapes, craggy coasts, and volcanic structures. Here are some of the best natural sites to discover on the island of Madeira:

Levadas

- ✓ **Description:** Irrigation ditches going back to the 15th century, currently function as picturesque hiking routes that traverse the island.
- ✓ **Highlights:** Walk along levadas such as Levada do Caldeirão Verde or Levada das 25 Fontes to explore waterfalls, woodlands, and indigenous vegetation.

Pico do Arieiro

- ✓ **Description:** Madeira's third-highest mountain, affording panoramic views of the island's rocky interior and shoreline.
- ✓ **Highlights:** Hike from Pico do Arieiro to Pico Ruivo, the highest mountain, for beautiful

panoramas and tough treks across the volcanic landscape.

São Lourenço Peninsula

- ✓ **Description:** A rough peninsula on Madeira's eastern point, famed for its stunning coastline cliffs and geological formations.
- ✓ **Highlights:** Walk the walk around the peninsula for stunning views of the Atlantic Ocean and the contrasting hues of the volcanic rocks.

Laurisilva Forest

- ✓ **Description:** A UNESCO World Heritage site includes ancient laurel trees that originally blanketed Southern Europe during the Tertiary era.
- ✓ **Highlights:** Explore paths like the Vereda da Encumeada or the Fanal Forest, home to rich vegetation, including rare species like the Madeira Laurel.

Porto Moniz Natural Swimming Pools

- ✓ **Description:** Natural rock pools filled with clean ocean water, generated by volcanic lava flows and tides.
- ✓ **Highlights:** Swim in the pools, surrounded by magnificent cliffs and ocean vistas, creating a unique natural swimming experience.

Curral das Freiras (Nun's Valley)

- ✓ **Description:** An isolated valley tucked in the center of Madeira, surrounded by high mountains.
- ✓ **Highlights:** Visit sites like Eira do Serrado for panoramic views of Curral das Freiras, famed for its quiet mood and magnificent panoramas.

Funchal Botanical Garden (Jardim Botânico)

- ✓ **Description:** A botanical garden overlooking Funchal, featuring a broad diversity of native and exotic plant species.
- ✓ **Highlights:** Stroll through themed gardens, featuring succulents, orchids, and tropical plants, with views of the city and port below.

These natural attractions in Madeira provide tourists an opportunity to see the island's different environments, from Rocky Mountains and old forests to stunning coasts and floral gardens. Whether you're trekking along levadas or resting in natural rock pools, Madeira's natural splendor delivers amazing experiences for nature lovers and adventurers alike.

Hiking and Outdoor Activities

Madeira is a destination for trekking and outdoor sports, with different landscapes that vary from steep mountains to lush woods and stunning seaside cliffs. Here are some of the top hiking paths and outdoor activities to enjoy on the island:

Levada Walks

- ✓ **Description:** Follow the ancient irrigation systems (levadas) that crisscross the island, giving magnificent routes through woods, valleys, and along mountainsides.
- ✓ **Highlights:** Popular levada treks include Levada do Caldeirão Verde, Levada das 25 Fontes, and Levada do Rei, each providing distinct landscapes and vistas.

Pico Ruivo

- **Description:** The highest summit on Madeira, reachable by a tough but rewarding walk from Pico do Arieiro or Achada do Teixeira.
- **Highlights:** Enjoy panoramic views of the island's central mountain range and shoreline from the peak of Pico Ruivo, typically cloaked in mist and fog.

Vereda da Ponta de São Lourenço

- **Description:** A picturesque route around the eastern extremity of Madeira's São Lourenço Peninsula, notable for its rough shoreline and geological formations.
- **Highlights:** Walk along cliffs overlooking the Atlantic Ocean, passing through colorful volcanic rocks and enjoying views of Ilhéu da Cevada.

Laurisilva Forest Trails

- **Description:** Explore the ancient laurel woods (Laurisilva), a UNESCO World Heritage site, with paths like Vereda da Encumeada or the Fanal Forest.

Highlights: Discover indigenous flora, like Madeira Laurel and moss-covered trees, among a tranquil and biodiverse setting.

Mountain Biking

- ✓ **Description:** Ride around Madeira's various landscapes, from tough mountain paths to lovely seaside routes.
- ✓ **Highlights:** Explore routes like the Achada do Teixeira to Pico Ruivo descent or the Ponta de São Lourenço loop, giving exhilarating descents and stunning vistas.

Canyoning

- ✓ **Description:** Navigate through Madeira's canyons and waterfalls, mixing hiking, rappelling, and swimming.
- ✓ **Highlights:** Experience adrenaline-pumping descents over natural rock formations and dive into crystal-clear pools among lush flora.

Scuba Diving and Snorkeling

- ✓ **Description:** Discover Madeira's underwater wonderland, noted for its pristine waters, volcanic structures, and abundant marine life.
- ✓ **Highlights:** Dive locations include Garajau Marine Park and Porto Moniz natural pools, allowing possibilities to explore colorful fish, caverns, and shipwrecks.

Paragliding

- ✓ **Description:** Soar over Madeira's sceneries, taking in panoramic vistas of mountains, shorelines, and towns.
- ✓ **Highlights:** Experience tandem flights from spots like Pico do Arieiro or Madeira's north coast, getting a bird's-eye perspective of the island's natural splendor.

These hiking and outdoor activities in Madeira are offered to explorers and nature lovers wishing to explore the island's different landscapes and enjoy its natural beauty up close. Whether you're trekking along levadas, swimming into natural springs, or flying over gorgeous panoramas, Madeira provides unique outdoor experiences for all levels of expertise.

Local Food and Wine

Madeira's food is a delicious combination of Portuguese tastes with distinct regional delicacies, enhanced by locally made wines. Here's a guide to sampling the native cuisine and wine of Madeira:

Local Dishes and Specialties

Espetada

- ✓ **Description:** Skewers of marinated beef or pig, cooked over an open flame and seasoned with garlic and bay leaves.
- ✓ **Where to Find:** Enjoy Espetada at traditional restaurants and taverns around Madeira, frequently served with Milho Frito (fried corn) and salad.

Bolo do Caco

- ✓ **Description:** Madeiran flatbread prepared with sweet potato, grilled on a hot stone, and generally eaten with garlic butter.

- ✓ **Where to Find:** Taste Bolo do Caco in local markets, street sellers, and restaurants, commonly served as a side dish or with traditional fillings like beef or chorizo.

Black Scabbardfish (Espada)

- ✓ **Description:** A local fish delicacy, commonly served with banana and passion fruit sauce, or grilled with garlic and olive oil.
- ✓ **Where to Find:** Try Espada at seaside restaurants and seafood diners, combined with local veggies and rice.
- ✓ **Lapas**
- ✓ **Description:** Grilled limpets, a favorite shellfish snack in Madeira, generally served with garlic butter and lemon.
- ✓ **Where to Find:** Look for Lapas at seaside towns and seafood restaurants, enjoyed as an appetizer or light dinner.

Sopa de Tomate e Cebola

- ✓ **Description:** Madeira's rendition of tomato and onion soup, seasoned with local herbs and served hot or cold.
- ✓ **Where to Find:** Sample Sopa de Tomate e Cebola at traditional diners and family-run restaurants, accompanied with bread and local olive oil.

Local Desserts & Sweets

Bolo de Mel

- ✓ **Description:** Madeira honey cake, rich in spices, almonds, and molasses, is commonly relished during festive events.
- ✓ **Where to Find:** Taste Bolo de Mel at bakeries and cafés around Madeira, served with a cup of Madeira wine.

Queijadas da Madeira

- ✓ **Description:** Small cheese tarts cooked with fresh cheese, sugar, and eggs, with a touch of cinnamon and lemon zest.

- ✓ **Where to Find:** Look for Queijadas da Madeira at local pastry shops and marketplaces, excellent for a sweet snack or dessert.

Local Wines

Madeira Wine

- ✓ **Description:** A fortified wine made solely on the island of Madeira, recognized for its many styles including dry, medium-dry, medium-sweet, and sweet.
- ✓ **Varieties:** Explore Madeira wine kinds such as Sercial (dry), Verdelho (medium-dry), Bual (medium-sweet), and Malmsey (sweet), each giving distinct tastes and characteristics.

Poncha

- ✓ **Description:** A typical Madeiran drink prepared with aguardente (distilled alcohol), honey, lemon juice, and sugar, frequently flavored with fruit such as passion fruit or tangerine.
- ✓ **Where to Find:** Enjoy Poncha at local pubs and taverns, particularly in coastal towns and tourist regions, served cold or over ice.

Dining Experiences

- ✓ **Traditional Tascas and Restaurants:** Visit small tascas (taverns) and family-run eateries to experience genuine Madeiran food and wines in a pleasant and inviting ambiance.
- ✓ **Local Markets:** Explore fresh vegetables, seafood, and artisanal items at markets like Mercado dos Lavradores in Funchal, where you can sample local delicacies and purchase things to take home.
- ✓ **Festivals & Events:** Attend culinary festivals and cultural events in Madeira, such as the Madeira Wine Festival or the Feast of Our Lady of Monte, to sample traditional cuisine and wines among exuberant festivities.

Enjoying the native cuisine and wine of Madeira is not only about tastes but also about immersing yourself in the island's rich culinary tradition and friendly welcome. Whether you're eating in a charming restaurant or enjoying street cuisine at a market, Madeira provides a gastronomic adventure that thrills the senses and represents its cultural character.

Festivals and Events

Madeira organizes a range of exciting festivals and events throughout the year, honoring its cultural history, customs, and natural beauty. Here are some of the important festivals and events to enjoy in Madeira:

Madeira Carnival

- ✓ **Description:** A boisterous carnival event including parades, music, dancing, and bright costumes.
- ✓ **Highlights:** Join the celebrations in Funchal and other towns around Madeira, with street parties, masked balls, and performances.

Madeira Flower Festival (Festa da Flor)

- ✓ **Description:** A floral spectacle honoring spring with flower carpets, parades, and exhibits.
- ✓ **Highlights:** Admire floral displays across Funchal, including the famed flower carpets created of native blossoms, and participate in concerts and cultural activities.

Madeira Wine Festival (Festa do Vinho)

- ✓ **Description:** A celebration of Madeira wine, with wine tastings, parades, and traditional grape harvest rites.
- ✓ **Highlights:** Attend wine-related activities in Funchal and neighboring vineyards, including the historical recreation of grape pressing and the chance to sample several kinds of Madeira wine.

Atlantic Festival

- ✓ **Description:** A month-long event in June commemorating Madeira's culture with music concerts, folklore performances, and fireworks displays.
- ✓ **Highlights:** Enjoy open-air performances in Praça do Povo in Funchal, witness the International Fireworks Competition, and enjoy traditional dances and music from Madeira.

Christmas and New Year Celebrations

- ✓ **Description:** Festive festivities between December and January, include Christmas markets, concerts, and the iconic New Year's Eve fireworks show.

- ✓ **Highlights:** Visit Funchal's adorned streets and squares, attend religious processions, and join residents and visitors for the stunning fireworks display over the bay.

Columbus Festival

- ✓ **Description:** Commemorates the island's link to Christopher Columbus, incorporating exhibits, street markets, and cultural events.
- ✓ **Highlights:** Explore historical displays and enjoy celebrations in Porto Santo and other areas related to Columbus's travels.

Festival of Our Lady of Monte (Nossa Senhora do Monte)

- ✓ **Description:** A religious and cultural event celebrating the patron saint of Madeira, including processions, church services, and traditional music.
- ✓ **Highlights:** Witness the procession of Our Lady of Monte from Funchal Cathedral to Monte Church, accompanied by local folklore groups and music bands.

Cultural and Sporting Events

- ✓ **Description:** Throughout the year, Madeira holds a range of cultural events, including music festivals, art exhibits, and athletic contests such as the Madeira Island Ultra Trail.

These festivals and events reflect Madeira's unique culture, traditions, and natural beauty, allowing visitors a chance to immerse themselves in local rituals and festivities throughout the year. Whether you're attending a flower procession, drinking Madeira wine, or watching fireworks over Funchal Harbor, Madeira's festivals guarantee remarkable experiences and an insight into its distinct island personality.

Chapter Five: Accommodations
Hotels and Resorts

In Portugal, you'll discover a broad choice of hotels and resorts catering to various interests, from opulent beachfront resorts to quaint boutique hotels. Here's an idea of the sorts of lodgings you may anticipate throughout different regions:

Types of Hotels and Resorts in Portugal

Luxury Resorts

- ✓ **Description:** Upscale hotels with premium facilities such as spas, several dining choices, golf courses, and private beach access.
- ✓ **Where to Find:** Algarve area (e.g., Quinta do Lago, Vilamoura), Lisbon (e.g., Cascais, Estoril), and Porto (e.g., Vila Nova de Gaia).

Boutique Hotels

- ✓ **Description:** Small, fashionable hotels with distinctive décor and individual service, frequently situated in historic buildings or attractive places.

- ✓ **Where to Find:** Lisbon (e.g., Bairro Alto, Chiado), Porto (e.g., Ribeira, Cedofeita), and rural districts (e.g., Douro Valley, Sintra).

Beachfront Hotels

- ✓ **Description:** Hotels positioned right on or near the beach, giving beautiful ocean views and convenient access to water sports and coastal activities.
- ✓ **Where to Find:** Algarve (e.g., Albufeira, Lagos), Madeira (e.g., Funchal, Porto Santo), and coastal towns near Lisbon (e.g., Cascais, Estoril).

Historic Pousadas

- ✓ **Description:** Unique lodgings are frequently built in ancient structures such as castles, monasteries, or palaces, giving a combination of tradition and contemporary luxury.
- ✓ **Where to Find:** Throughout Portugal, including Lisbon (e.g., Pousada de Lisboa), Porto (e.g., Pousada do Porto), and rural regions (e.g., Pousada de Óbidos, Pousada de Guimarães).

Rural Retreats

- ✓ **Description:** Tranquil lodgings are nestled in rural environments, giving a relaxing retreat with chances for hiking, wine tasting, and discovering local culture.
- ✓ **Where to Find:** Douro Valley (e.g., Quinta do Crasto), Alentejo area (e.g., Évora, Monsaraz), and northern Portugal (e.g., Gerês National Park).

City Center Hotels

- ✓ **Description:** Convenient lodgings situated in the middle of major cities, allowing easy access to cultural activities, restaurants, and nightlife.
- ✓ **Where to Find:** Lisbon (e.g., Baixa, Chiado), Porto (e.g., Ribeira, Aliados), and Coimbra (e.g., Historic Center).

All-Inclusive Resorts

- ✓ **Description:** Resorts provide extensive packages that include lodgings, food, beverages, and activities, excellent for families and tourists seeking convenience.

✓ **Where to Find:** Algarve (e.g., Albufeira, Vilamoura), Madeira (e.g., Funchal), and certain coastal regions near Lisbon.

Booking Tips

✓ **Seasonal Variations:** Portugal is popular in summer, particularly in coastal locations. Book well in advance during the busy season.

✓ **Reviews and Recommendations:** Check internet reviews and travel guides to identify lodgings that meet your interests and budget.

✓ **Local Charm:** Consider staying in boutique hotels or ancient pousadas for a distinct Portuguese experience.

Whether you like luxurious resorts by the beach, beautiful boutique hotels in ancient towns, or calm rural getaways, Portugal provides a broad selection of lodgings to meet all traveler's interests and tastes.

Budget-Friendly Options

For budget-conscious tourists visiting Portugal, there are lots of economical lodging alternatives that give comfort and convenience without breaking the bank. Here are some budget-friendly solutions to consider:

Budget-Friendly Accommodation Options in Portugal

Hostels

- ✓ **Description:** Dormitory-style or private rooms with communal amenities including baths and kitchens. Ideal for lone travelers or parties wishing to interact.
- ✓ **Where to Find:** Major cities like Lisbon, Porto, and Faro provide a range of hostels in key areas. Some coastal towns and rural regions also provide hostel lodgings.

Guesthouses and Pensiones

- ✓ **Description:** Small, family-run enterprises providing modest accommodations with minimum facilities. Often cheaper than hotels with a personal touch.
- ✓ **Where to Find:** Throughout Portugal, notably in urban areas and smaller towns. Look for opportunities in historic districts or residential neighborhoods.

Budget Hotels

- ✓ **Description:** Basic hotels provide necessary facilities like private rooms, en-suite bathrooms, and occasionally breakfast included. Often more inexpensive than mid-range or luxury hotels.
- ✓ **Where to Find:** In cities like Lisbon, Porto, and Coimbra, as well as near key transit hubs and tourist sites.

Airbnb and Vacation Rentals

- ✓ **Description:** Private apartments or rooms leased out by local hosts, allowing flexibility and frequently greater space and facilities compared to typical hotels.
- ✓ **Where to Find:** Available in Portugal, notably in metropolitan areas and important tourist attractions. Look for solutions that meet your price and geographical preferences.

Campgrounds and Eco-Lodges

- ✓ **Description:** Affordable lodging alternatives for outdoor enthusiasts, including campsites, cabins, or eco-friendly resorts in natural locations.

- ✓ **Where to Find:** Near national parks, coastal locations, and rural regions like the Azores and Alentejo. Facilities vary from basic to highly equipped sites with amenities.

Tips for Budget Travelers

- ✓ **Book in Advance:** Especially during high tourist seasons (summer and big holidays) to ensure the greatest pricing and availability.
- ✓ **Explore Alternative Locations:** Consider staying somewhat outside city centers or in lesser-known districts for reduced pricing.
- ✓ **Use Travel Apps and Websites:** Compare rates and read reviews on platforms like Booking.com, Hostelworld, Airbnb, and TripAdvisor to get the best discounts.
- ✓ **Local Recommendations:** Ask locals or hosts for budget-friendly eating alternatives and activities to make the most of your vacation without overpaying.

By picking budget-friendly lodgings in Portugal, you may stretch your vacation budget while still enjoying the rich culture, magnificent scenery, and wonderful food that this lovely nation has to offer.

Unique Stays

If you're seeking unique and unforgettable housing experiences in Portugal, various possibilities offer something out of the usual. Here are some unusual stays to consider:

Historic Pousadas

- ✓ **Description:** Stay in ancient structures such as castles, monasteries, and palaces turned into attractive hotels.
- ✓ **Highlights:** Experience Portugal's tradition with contemporary amenities, frequently in gorgeous locales. Examples include Pousada de Óbidos, Pousada de Guimarães, and Pousada de Lisboa.

Quinta Stays

- ✓ **Description:** Stay at a quinta, a classic Portuguese estate or farmland, giving a rustic and unique experience.

✓ **Highlights:** Enjoy vineyard accommodations in the Douro Valley, olive farm stays in Alentejo, or citrus orchard stays in the Algarve, frequently with possibilities for wine sampling or farm-to-table eating.

Windmill or Lighthouse Stays

✓ **Description:** Stay in a renovated windmill or lighthouse, giving unusual lodgings with panoramic views.

✓ **Highlights:** Examples include windmill stays in the Azores or lighthouse stays along the Portuguese coastline, giving a combination of history and visual beauty.

Treehouse Accommodations

✓ **Description:** Stay in a treehouse situated in the Portuguese countryside or woodland regions.

✓ **Highlights:** Experience nature up close with treehouse stays in areas like Serra da Estrela or Peneda-Gerês National Park, giving a quiet and eco-friendly refuge.

Houseboats

- ✓ **Description:** Stay aboard a houseboat or floating lodging, giving a unique view of Portugal's rivers or coastal locations.
- ✓ **Highlights:** Experience a floating stay in sites like Aveiro's canals or along the Douro River, mixing leisure with waterfront vistas and nautical flair.

Cave Dwellings

- ✓ **Description:** Stay in a cave home or troglodyte accommodation, giving a cool hideaway in hot months.
- ✓ **Highlights:** Experience cave stays in regions like the Algarve coast or Alentejo region, delivering a unique combination of old life and contemporary luxury.

Tips for Booking Unique Stays

- ✓ **Research and Plan Ahead:** Unique lodgings might be in great demand, particularly during peak seasons. Book well in advance to ensure your desired dates.

- ✓ **Check Reviews and facilities:** Ensure that the unique stay delivers the facilities and experiences you're searching for by reading reviews and reviewing specifics on booking sites.
- ✓ **Take Accordingly:** Depending on the particular accommodation, you may need to take special goods such as hiking gear for treehouses or beachwear for houseboats.
- ✓ **Embrace the Experience:** Unique stays give you a chance to make lasting memories and immerse yourself in Portugal's culture and natural beauty in a particular manner.

By picking a unique lodging in Portugal, you may enrich your vacation experience with remarkable stays that provide both comfort and a feeling of adventure.

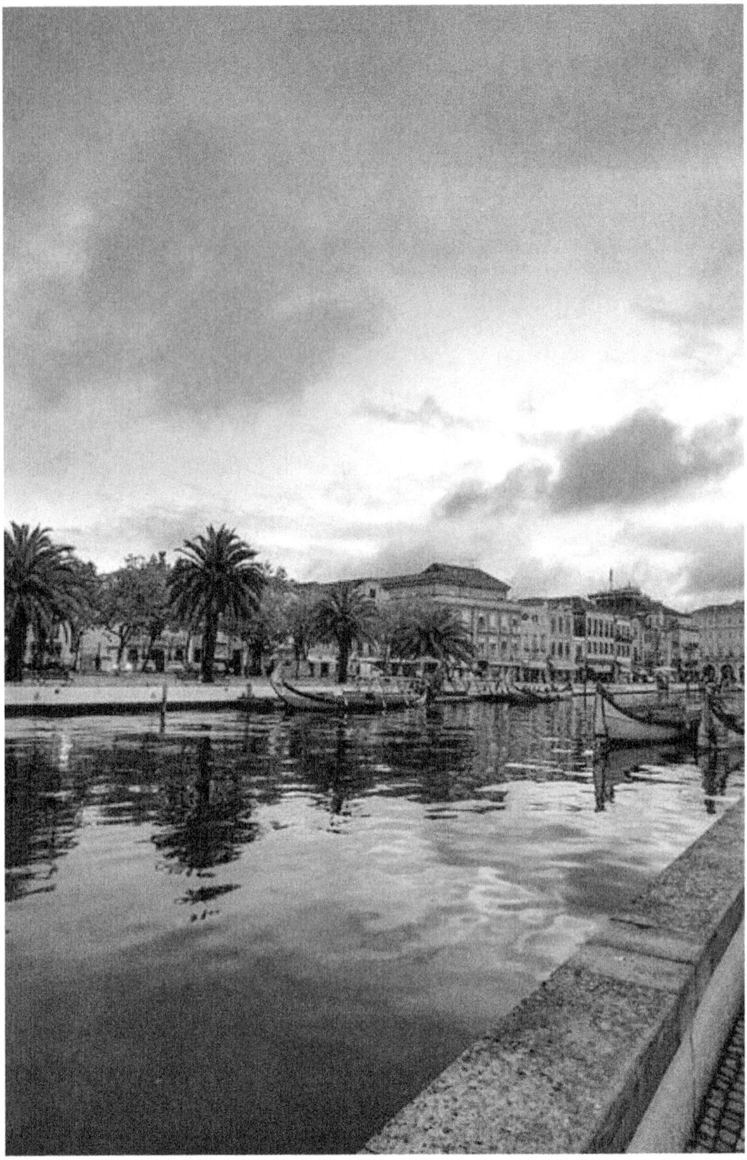

Chapter Six: Getting Around Portugal

Public Transportation

Public transportation in Portugal is a simple and effective method to see cities and commute across regions. Here's a full breakdown of the key public transit alternatives available:

Metro

- ✓ **Lisbon Metro:** The Lisbon Metro (Metropolitano de Lisboa) serves Lisbon and its suburbs with four lines (blue, yellow, green, and red). It's efficient for going about the city core and important attractions.
- ✓ **Porto Metro:** The Porto Metro (Metro do Porto) runs six lines (A, B, C, D, E, and F), linking Porto, Matosinhos, Maia, Vila do Conde and other adjacent municipalities. It's handy for traveling inside Porto and the Greater Porto region.

Trams and Funiculars

- ✓ **Lisbon Trams:** Lisbon is famed for its ancient trams, particularly Tram 28, which goes through the city's old districts, affording magnificent vistas. Tram 15 also operates along the Belém region.
- ✓ **Porto Trams:** Porto features trams that link downtown regions with the riverbank and other picturesque sites, such as Tram 1 (Passeio Alegre to Infante).
- ✓ **Funiculars:** Lisbon and Porto feature funiculars (Ascensores) that enable travel between lower and higher areas of steep districts. Examples include Elevador da Glória and Elevador da Bica in Lisbon, and Funicular dos Guindais in Porto.

Buses

- ✓ **City Buses:** Both Lisbon and Porto have significant bus networks managed by Carris (Lisbon) and STCP (Porto), servicing numerous routes throughout the cities and outlying districts.

Intercity Buses: Rede Expressos is the largest intercity bus operator in Portugal, linking major cities and communities throughout the nation. It's a cheap method to travel across locations.

Trains

- ✓ **Comboios de Portugal (CP):** CP runs rail services across Portugal, including suburban trains (Urbanos) in Lisbon and Porto, regional trains, and long-distance trains (Intercidades and Alfa Pendular).
- ✓ **Lisbon Suburban Trains:** CP runs suburban trains (Linha de Sintra, Linha de Cascais, etc.) linking Lisbon with adjacent cities like Sintra, Cascais, and Setúbal.
- ✓ **Porto Suburban Trains:** CP runs suburban trains (Linha de Aveiro, Linha de Braga, etc.) linking Porto with adjacent towns and cities.

Ferry and Boat Services

- ✓ **Lisbon Ferry:** Ferries run over the Tagus River, linking Lisbon (Cais do Sodré) with Cacilhas, Trafaria, and Montijo.

- ✓ **Other Ferry Services:** Ferry services also link Porto with Vila Nova de Gaia across the Douro River.

Ticketing and Payment

- ✓ **Viva Viagem Card:** This rechargeable card is used for metro, trams, buses, and certain trains in Lisbon. It may be bought and topped up at stations and kiosks.
- ✓ **Andante Card:** In Porto, the Andante card is used for metro, trams, buses, and suburban trains. It's offered in metro stations and Andante outlets.
- ✓ **Single Tickets:** Single trip tickets are also available for metro, trams, buses, and trains if you choose not to use a card.

Tips for Using Public Transportation

- ✓ **Plan Ahead:** Check timetables and routes online or with mobile applications like CP, Carris, or STCP.
- ✓ **Validate Tickets:** Remember to validate tickets before entering trams, buses, or trains when necessary.

- ✓ **Keep Tickets:** Hold onto your ticket or card until the conclusion of your voyage, since inspections are periodically undertaken.

Public transportation in Portugal is typically secure, dependable, and economical, making it a good alternative for visitors touring cities and trekking into the country's attractive areas.

Renting a Car

Renting a vehicle in Portugal is a terrific alternative for tourists wishing to explore the nation at their speed, particularly outside major towns and tourist hotspots. Here's a thorough guide on hiring a vehicle in Portugal:

Requirements

- ✓ **Minimum Age:** Generally, the minimum age to hire an automobile in Portugal is 21 years old. Drivers under 25 may suffer a young driver surcharge.
- ✓ **Driver's License:** A valid driver's license from your country of residence is necessary. International Driving Permits (IDP) are encouraged but not usually needed.

Booking

- ✓ **Booking in Advance:** It's preferable to reserve your rental vehicle in advance, particularly during busy tourist seasons (summer and major holidays), to get the greatest pricing and availability.
- ✓ **Comparison:** Compare rental pricing, terms, and conditions from multiple providers (local and worldwide) to discover the best offer. Websites like Rentalcars.com, Kayak, and Auto Europe are excellent for evaluating possibilities.

Pick-Up

- ✓ **Locations Airports:** Most major airports in Portugal, such as Lisbon Portela Airport (LIS) and Porto Airport (OPO), offer various car rental firms present onsite.
- ✓ **City Centers:** Car rental agencies are also accessible in city centers and major rail terminals. Confirm the pick-up location when booking your appointment.

Types of Cars

- ✓ **Car Categories:** Rental businesses provide a choice of vehicles including small cars, sedans, SUVs, and even specialist vehicles like convertibles or luxury automobiles.
- ✓ **Gearbox:** Most rental vehicles in Portugal have manual gearboxes (stick shift). Automatic automobiles are available but may be restricted and more costly.

Insurance

- ✓ **Basic Insurance:** Rental prices normally include basic insurance (Collision Damage Waiver - CDW and Theft Protection), however it sometimes comes with an excess (deductible).
- ✓ **Additional Coverage:** Consider acquiring additional insurance coverage to minimize or eliminate the excess, such as the Super Collision Damage Waiver (Super CDW) or Personal Accident Insurance (PAI).

Driving Tips

- ✓ **Driving Laws:** Familiarize yourself with Portugal's driving laws and regulations, including speed limits, road signs, and parking requirements.
- ✓ **Tolls:** Some roads in Portugal (Autoestradas) are tolled. Rental vehicles may have electronic toll devices (Via Verde) or you may pay at toll booths (typically indicated with green flags).
- ✓ **Parking:** Use paid parking lots (parques) or metered street parking (zona azul) in cities. Avoid parking illegally to avoid penalties or towing.

Fuel

- ✓ **Fuel Types:** Gasoline (gasolina) and diesel (gasóleo) are readily accessible. Check your rental car's gasoline type before refilling.
- ✓ **Gas Stations:** Look for big gas station chains including Galp, BP, and Repsol. Many stations are self-service, taking cash or credit cards.

Navigation

- ✓ **GPS:** Consider renting a GPS device or utilizing a mobile GPS app with offline maps to navigate, particularly in rural locations where signage may be sparse.
- ✓ **Cell Data:** Purchase a local SIM card or verify your cell plan includes data for navigation and communication.

Benefits of Renting a Car

- ✓ **Flexibility:** Explore off-the-beaten-path locations and picturesque highways in your own time.
- ✓ **Convenience:** Easily reach rural locations, beaches, and natural parks that may not be well-served by public transit.
- ✓ **Comfort:** Enjoy comfort and solitude when traveling with family or friends, with adequate room for bags and personal things.

Renting a vehicle in Portugal allows the opportunity to see the country's various landscapes, ancient cities, and hidden jewels outside the regular tourist itineraries.

With correct preparation and awareness of local driving conditions, it may improve your vacation experience and allow for exciting road excursions around Portugal.

Biking and Walking

Exploring Portugal by bicycling and walking gives a more personal and relaxed approach to discovering its various landscapes, beautiful villages, and cultural sites. Here's a handbook on riding and walking in Portugal:

Biking

Popular Regions for Biking

- ✓ **Algarve:** Coastal roads with stunning vistas, including pathways along cliffs and beaches.
- ✓ **Douro Valley:** Vineyard scenery along the Douro River, with pathways linking wine estates.
- ✓ **Alentejo:** Rolling plains and cork oak woodlands, suitable for cycling through charming communities.
- ✓ **Azores:** The volcanic landscape provides tough hikes and coastline walks on various islands.

Types of Biking Routes

- ✓ **Bicycle Trails:** Dedicated bicycle lanes and trails in national parks, woodlands, and along coastal roads.
- ✓ **Road Cycling:** Scenic itineraries on rural roads and coastal highways, appropriate for road cycles.
- ✓ **Mountain Biking:** Trails in hilly places like Serra da Estrela and Peneda-Gerês National Park, provide demanding terrain.

Bike Rental and Tours

- ✓ **Rental Shops:** Available in major cities and tourist locations. Check for businesses selling excellent bikes and safety equipment.
- ✓ **Guided excursions:** Join scheduled bicycle excursions with local guides, giving insights into culture and history along the way.

Useful Tips

- ✓ **Safety Gear:** Wear helmets and high-visibility gear. Carry a repair kit, water, and food for extended journeys.

- ✓ **Weather:** Check weather conditions and plan rides appropriately, particularly in mountainous places where weather might change suddenly.
- ✓ **Local Regulations:** Observe traffic restrictions, defer to pedestrians, and respect natural protection zones.

Walking in Portugal

Scenic Routes for Walking

- ✓ **Historic Centers:** Explore small alleyways and cobblestone lanes in Lisbon, Porto, and Coimbra.
- ✓ **Coastal Trails:** Walk over cliffs and sandy beaches on the Costa Vicentina or Algarve coast.
- ✓ **Mountain Hikes:** Trekking paths in Serra da Estrela, Madeira, and Azores for panoramic views and ecological immersion.

Popular Walking Trails

- ✓ **Rota Vicentina:** Long-distance track in Alentejo and Algarve, including coastal and rural routes.

- ✓ **Camino Português:** Pilgrimage path from Lisbon to Santiago de Compostela, going through ancient cities and landscapes.
- ✓ **Levadas of Madeira:** Irrigation ditches turned into hiking pathways, traveling through lush woods and hilly terrain.

Walking Tips

- ✓ **Footwear:** Wear durable, comfortable shoes suited for various terrains, particularly for walks in hilly places.
- ✓ **Water & food:** Carry adequate water and food, particularly for longer walks where amenities may be scarce.
- ✓ **Local Guidance:** Use trail maps, and guidebooks, or join guided walking excursions for safety and local insights.

Additional Considerations

- ✓ **Accommodations:** Plan accommodations along your trip, whether in cities, guesthouses, or rural lodgings.

- ✓ **Permits and Fees:** Some natural parks or protected places may demand permits or admission fees for hiking or riding.
- ✓ **Seasonal Variations:** Consider weather conditions and seasonal closures, particularly for high-altitude climbs or seaside paths prone to strong winds.

Exploring Portugal by bicycle and walking enables you to immerse yourself in its natural beauty, cultural legacy, and local communities at a slow pace. Whether you select seaside walks, medieval trails, or mountain climbs, each route gives a distinct view of Portugal's various landscapes and rich history.

Tips for Driving in Portugal

Driving in Portugal may be a wonderful way to discover the country's different landscapes and historic attractions. Here are some basic suggestions to guarantee a safe and happy driving experience:

Documentation and Requirements

- **Driver's License:** Carry a valid driver's license from your country of residence. An International Driving Permit (IDP) is recommended but not usually needed.
- **Insurance:** Ensure your rental car or own vehicle is appropriately insured. Basic insurance (CDW - Collision Damage Waiver) is often included, however, consider extra coverage to lower excess (deductible).

Vehicle paperwork: Carry vehicle registration (V5C), insurance paperwork, and rental agreement (if applicable) in the car at all times.

Road Rules and Regulations

- **Drive on the Right:** Traffic in Portugal drives on the right-hand side of the road.
- **Speed Limits:** Standard speed limits are 50 km/h in urban areas, 90 km/h on rural roads, and 120 km/h on highways (unless otherwise specified).

- ✓ **Seat Belts:** Seat belts are necessary for all passengers, and children must use proper child seats or restraints.
- ✓ **Mobile Phones:** The use of portable mobile phones while driving is illegal. Use hands-free devices if required.

Road Conditions

- ✓ **Highways (Autoestradas):** Toll highways (marked with blue flags) link major cities and tourist sites. Some tolls are electronic (Via Verde) or demand payment at booths.
- ✓ **Secondary Roads:** Rural roads (EN - Estrada Nacional) may be smaller and twisting. Exercise care, particularly in hilly or coastal locations.
- ✓ **Parking:** Follow local parking restrictions. Paid parking (parques) and metered street parking (zona azul) are widespread in cities. Avoid unlawful parking to save penalties or towing.

Navigation with GPS

✓ **GPS navigating:** Use a GPS device or smartphone app with offline maps for navigating. Ensure your mobile data plan supports use overseas.

Road Signs: Familiarize yourself with Portuguese road signs, which employ international symbols and may contain local variants.

Fuel and Services

✓ **Fuel Types:** Gasoline (gasolina) and diesel (gasóleo) are generally accessible at gas stations (postos de abastecimento). Check your vehicle's fuel type before refilling.

✓ **Service Stations:** Look for large chains like Galp, BP, and Repsol. Many stations are self-service and take cash or credit cards.

Driving Etiquette

✓ **Overtaking:** Only overtake on the left. Use turn signals (indicators) to express your intentions.

- ✓ **Roundabouts:** Yield to vehicles already in the roundabout. Traffic within the roundabout has the right of way.
- ✓ **Pedestrians:** Yield to pedestrians at crosswalks (passadeiras). Failure to do so might result in sanctions.

Emergencies

- ✓ **Emergency Numbers:** Dial 112 for emergencies (police, fire, medical aid) across Portugal.
- ✓ **Breakdowns:** In case of a vehicle breakdown, use danger lights and install a warning triangle (triângulo de pré-sinalização) behind your car. Contact your rental company or roadside help.

Additional Tips

- ✓ **Plan Routes:** Plan your routes, particularly for longer excursions. Consider taking scenic routes and avoiding peak traffic periods in large cities.
- ✓ **Local information:** Ask locals or your hotel for information on driving conditions, road closures, and preferred routes.

- ✓ **Stay Alert:** Portugal's different landscapes might provide unforeseen obstacles. Stay careful, particularly in remote or hilly places.

By following these suggestions and being conscious of local norms and circumstances, you may have a safe and enjoyable driving experience while seeing the beauty and cultural diversity of Portugal.

Chapter Seven: Practical Information

Safety and Health

When going to Portugal, it's crucial to prioritize your safety and health to guarantee a smooth and pleasurable journey. Here are some advice and information on safety and health considerations:

Safety Tips

General Safety: Portugal is typically a safe nation for tourists. Use common sense measures, such as securing valuables and being mindful of your surroundings, particularly in popular tourist locations.

Emergency Numbers:

> ➢ **Emergency services:** Dial 112 for police, fire, or medical emergencies across Portugal.

Scams and Pickpocketing: Be aware of fraud, especially in tourist-heavy regions. Keep your possessions safe and avoid exhibiting big quantities of cash or precious objects.

Natural Hazards: Portugal is prone to forest fires, particularly during the dry summer months. Follow local news and cautions while going to rural or wooded regions.

Driving Safety: If hiring a vehicle, educate yourself about local traffic regulations and road conditions. Portugal drives on the right-hand side of the road.

Health Tips Travel Insurance: Ensure you have adequate travel insurance that covers medical expenditures, including emergency evacuation.

Medical Facilities: Medical facilities in Portugal are typically of a high grade, especially in big towns like Lisbon and Porto. Pharmacies (farmácias) are frequently accessible and may give over-the-counter drugs.

Vaccinations: No special vaccines are necessary for entrance into Portugal. Ensure regular immunizations are up to date, including measles-mumps-rubella (MMR), diphtheria-tetanus-pertussis, varicella (chickenpox), polio, and influenza.

Water and Food Safety:

- ➤ Tap water in Portugal is typically safe to drink. However, bottled water is generally accessible and may be preferable, particularly in remote regions or for individuals with sensitive stomachs.
- ➤ Enjoy local cuisine but take care with seafood and ensure it's from trustworthy suppliers, particularly in coastal places.

Sun Protection: Portugal has a Mediterranean climate with sunny weather, particularly in summer. Use sunscreen, wear protective clothes, and remain hydrated to avoid sunburn and

Additional Tips

- ➤ **Local Laws and Customs:** Respect local traditions and regulations, including clothing rules for religious places and photography prohibitions in specific locations.
- ➤ **Travel Advisory Updates:** Check for any travel advisories or updates from your government for Portugal, particularly regarding safety and health.

By following these safety and health precautions, you may ensure a safe and happy experience while touring the lovely nation of Portugal.

Packing Essentials

When packing for your vacation to Portugal, consider the following basics to ensure you have all you need for a comfortable and pleasurable journey:

Clothing and Accessories

Weather-Appropriate Clothing:

- **Summer (June to August):** Lightweight and breathable apparel such as shorts, t-shirts, dresses, and sandals. Don't forget a swimsuit if you want to visit beaches.
- **Spring and Autumn:** Layered clothes for various weather, including light jackets or sweaters.
- **Winter:** Warmer clothes, including jackets, scarves, and gloves, particularly for northern regions and hilly terrain.

Comfortable Footwear:

- Walking shoes or sneakers for touring and visiting places.
- Sandals or comfy shoes for warmer weather and beach activities.
- Dress shoes for nights or fancier eateries.

Rain Gear:

- Lightweight rain jacket or umbrella, particularly if traveling in spring or fall when rains are more common.

Travel Accessories Travel Documents:

- Passport or ID card (plus duplicates held separately).
- Travel itinerary, lodging arrangements, and any relevant visas or travel insurance paperwork.

Electronics:

- Smartphone and charger with an adaptor appropriate for European outlets.
- Camera or GoPro for capturing memories.
- Portable power bank for charging electronics on the move.

Health and Safety:

- Prescription drugs (with copies of prescriptions).
- First aid package containing necessities including pain medications, bandages, and antiseptic wipes.
- Hand sanitizer and face masks (given current health requirements).

Personal Items

Toiletries:

- Travel-sized toiletries (shampoo, conditioner, soap, toothbrush, etc.).
- Sunscreen and after-sun lotion for sun protection.

Personal Items:

- Sunglasses and cap for sun protection.
- Travel cushion and earplugs for comfort during flights or lengthy excursions.
- Travel handbook or maps for navigation and planning.

Miscellaneous Reusable

- **Water Bottle:** Stay hydrated with a refillable water bottle, particularly during warmer months.
- **Daypack or Backpack:** Lightweight bag for everyday travels to carry basics like water, food, and a camera.
- **Language Guide or Translator App:** Basic Portuguese words or a translating program to converse with locals.

Tips:

- **Pack Light:** Portugal's metropolitan regions offer contemporary conveniences, so you can simply acquire any forgotten things.
- **Check Airline Regulations:** Verify luggage limitations and restrictions before packing to avoid unnecessary expenses.
- **Seasonal Considerations:** Tailor your packing list to the precise season and activities planned for your vacation.

By bringing these necessities, you'll be well-prepared for your vacation in Portugal, whether you're touring towns, resting on beaches, or enjoying the stunning scenery.

Local Etiquette

Understanding local manners may substantially improve your experience when vacationing in Portugal. Here are some crucial etiquette guidelines to bear in mind:

General Etiquette

Greetings:

- Greetings are often warm and cordial. Shake hands while meeting someone for the first time.
- Use formal titles (such as "Senhor" for Mr. and "Senhora" for Mrs.) unless requested to use first names.

Punctuality: Punctuality is important for appointments and social meetings. Arrive on time or somewhat early.

Personal Space: Portuguese people cherish personal space. Maintain a reasonable distance during chats and prevent excessive physical touch.

Dining Etiquette Meals:

- Dining is a social event in Portugal. Enjoy leisurely lunches with friends and family.
- Wait for the host to start eating before you begin your meal.
- **Bread and Olives:** Bread and olives are usually offered as appetizers. It's polite to eat them.

Tipping: Tipping is not necessary but is appreciated for excellent service. A gratuity of roughly 5-10% is usual in restaurants.

Cultural Sensitivity Religion: Portugal is primarily Catholic. Respect religious norms and traditions, particularly while visiting churches or religious places.

Dress Code: Casual wear is normally appropriate, however, dress modestly while visiting religious institutions or premium restaurants.

Photography: Ask for permission before photographing individuals, particularly in rural regions or marketplaces. Respect privacy.

Language Language: Learn a few simple Portuguese words ("por favor" for please, "obrigado/a" for thank you) as a token of respect.

Social Customs

- **Fado Music:** Fado is a classic Portuguese music genre recognized for its gloomy tunes. Enjoy concerts politely in specified settings.
- **Gift Giving:** Small presents or mementos are welcomed when invited to someone's house.
- **Public Behavior:** Public expressions of love should be reasonable and mindful of local traditions.

Environmental Awareness

- **Nature & Environment:** Respect natural environments and use authorized pathways while hiking or touring parks.
- **Waste Disposal:** Recycle wherever feasible and dispose of rubbish ethically.

By obeying local manners and traditions, you'll not only fit in more easily but also demonstrate appreciation for Portuguese culture and hospitality. Enjoy your trips in Portugal!

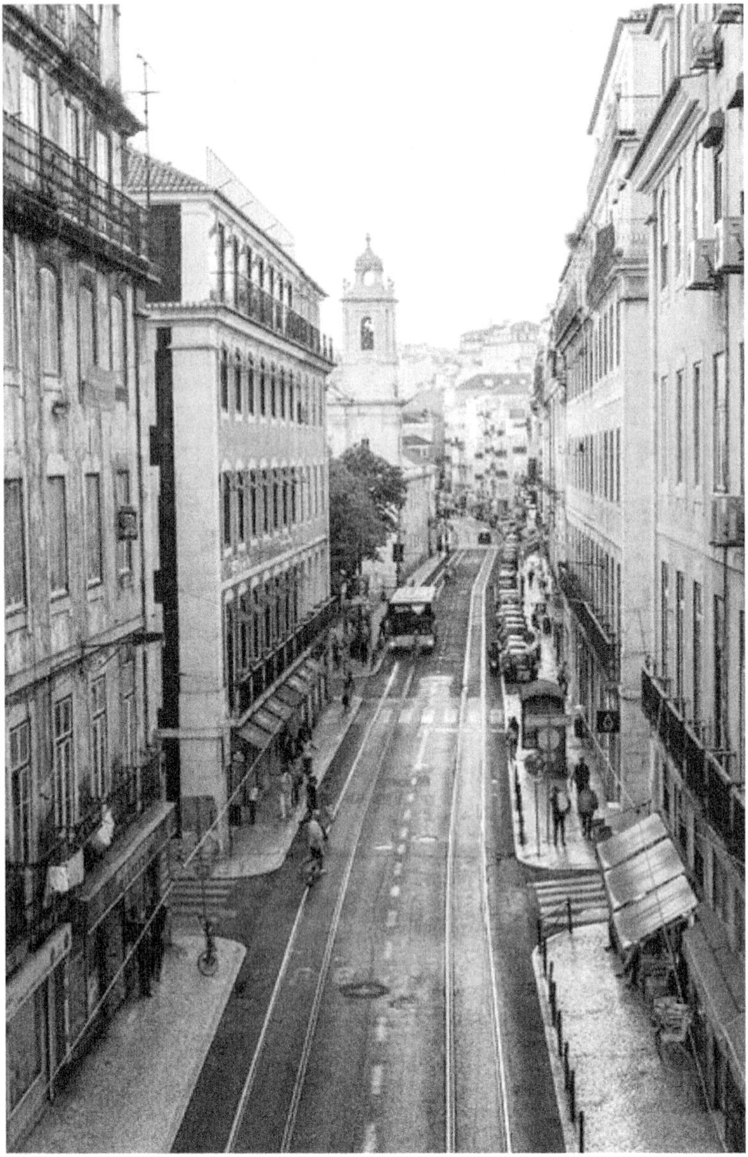

Chapter Eight: Sample Itineraries

3-Day Itinerary: Lisbon and Surroundings

Here's a 3-day itinerary centered on Lisbon and its surrounding locations, including both the city's cultural assets and regional attractions:

Day 1: Explore Lisbon

- **Morning:** Start with a visit to Belém. See the renowned Belém Tower and Jerónimos Monastery. Don't miss sampling the legendary Pastéis de Belém.
- **Afternoon:** Head back to downtown Lisbon and visit Baixa and Chiado. Visit Rossio Square and take a walk down Rua Augusta to Commerce Square (Praça do Comércio).
- **Evening:** Enjoy supper at a local restaurant in Bairro Alto or Alfama, followed by Fado music in Alfama's evocative venues.

Day 2: Sintra Day Trip

- **Morning:** Take a day excursion to Sintra. Start early to beat the crowds. Visit the fairy-tale Pena Palace,

Moorish Castle, and Quinta da Regaleira with its mysterious gardens and initiation well.
- **Afternoon:** Explore the historic town of Sintra, including the Sintra National Palace and its peculiar chimneys.
- **Evening:** Return to Lisbon and relax with supper at **a neighborhood restaurant or café.**

Day 3: Cascais and Estoril

- **Morning:** Head to Cascais. Visit the Boca do Inferno coastal cliffs and the picturesque Cascais Marina.
- **Afternoon:** Explore Estoril and its famed Casino Estoril, one of the biggest casinos in Europe. Relax at the gorgeous Tamariz Beach.
- **Evening:** Return to Lisbon. Spend your final evening seeing any missing attractions or having a goodbye supper at a favorite local eatery.

Tips for Your Trip

- **Transportation:** Use Lisbon's efficient metro, tram, and bus system for city exploration. Consider hiring a vehicle or joining guided excursions for day visits to Sintra, Cascais, and Estoril.

- **Tickets:** Purchase tickets in advance for major sights like Pena Palace and Belém Tower to avoid lengthy lineups.
- **Local Cuisine:** Don't miss sampling classic Portuguese delicacies like bacalhau (codfish), pastéis de nata (custard tarts), and grilled sardines.

This itinerary combines a balanced mix of Lisbon's dynamic city life and neighboring historical and scenic riches, ensuring you see the best of Lisbon and its surroundings in only three days.

7-Day Itinerary: Best of Portugal

Here's a complete 7-day itinerary to visit the attractions of Portugal, spanning Lisbon, Porto, the Douro Valley, and the Algarve:

Day 1: Arrival in Lisbon

- **Arrive in Lisbon:** Explore the ancient areas of Baixa and Alfama. Visit São Jorge Castle for panoramic views of the city.

- ➢ **Evening:** Enjoy a traditional Portuguese meal and Fado music in Alfama.

Day 2: Discovering Lisbon

- ➢ **Morning:** Visit the renowned Belém Tower and Jerónimos Monastery. Try the legendary Pastéis de Belém.
- ➢ **Afternoon:** Explore the contemporary architecture of Parque das Nações. Visit the Oceanarium and enjoy a cable car trip.
- ➢ **Evening:** Dinner at a local restaurant in Chiado or Bairro Alto.

Day 3: Day Trip to Sintra

- ➢ **Morning:** Head to Sintra. Visit the fairy-tale Pena Palace and the Moorish Castle. Explore the magical grounds of Quinta da Regaleira.
- ➢ **Afternoon:** Stroll around Sintra's historic center. Visit Sintra National Palace.

Evening: Return to Lisbon. Relax and have supper at Alfama or Baixa.

Day 4: Porto

- **Morning:** Travel to Porto (approximately 3 hours by rail or automobile).
- **Afternoon:** Explore the old heart of Porto (UNESCO World Heritage). Visit Clérigos Tower and Lello Bookstore.
- **Evening:** Dinner along the Douro River in Ribeira, savoring Porto's traditional food.

Day 5: Douro Valley Wine Region

- **Morning:** Take a picturesque drive or boat along the Douro River. Visit a Quinta (wine estate) for wine sampling.
- **Afternoon:** Explore lovely towns like Pinhão. Visit viewpoints for sweeping valley views.
- **Evening:** Return to Porto. Dinner at a neighborhood restaurant, possibly having some Porto wine.

Day 6: Algarve

- **Morning:** Fly to Faro or drive to the Algarve area (approximately 4 hours from Lisbon).
- **Afternoon:** Explore seaside cities like Lagos or Albufeira. Relax on gorgeous beaches.

Evening: Dinner at a seafood restaurant overlooking the Atlantic Ocean.

Day 7: Algarve Coast

- **Morning:** Discover the natural splendor of Ponta da Piedade and Cabo de São Vicente.
- **Afternoon:** Visit ancient cities like Tavira or Silves with its Moorish architecture.
- **Evening:** Return to Faro or Lisbon. Final evening to taste Portuguese food.

Tips for Your Trip:

- **Transportation:** Consider hiring a vehicle for flexibility, particularly for day excursions to Sintra, the Douro Valley, and the Algarve. Alternatively, utilize Portugal's efficient rail network for lengthier travels.
- **Tickets:** Book tickets in advance for popular destinations like Pena Palace, Douro Valley wine excursions, and flights to/from the Algarve.
- **Local Cuisine:** Indulge in regional delicacies like bacalhau (codfish), pastéis de nata (custard tarts), and fresh seafood meals throughout your vacation.

This itinerary provides a comprehensive experience of Portugal's cultural legacy, natural beauty, and gastronomic pleasures, ensuring you make the most of your 7-day visit to this enchanting nation.

10-Day Itinerary: In-Depth Exploration

For a more in-depth tour of Portugal over 10 days, you may explore major cities, historical monuments, natural landscapes, and cultural activities. Here's a full schedule to help you make the most of your trip:

Day 1-3: Lisbon

Day 1: Arrival in Lisbon

- **Arrive in Lisbon:** Transfer to your hotel and settle in.
- **Evening:** Explore surrounding areas like Baixa and Alfama. Visit São Jorge Castle for panoramic views.

Day 2: Lisbon Exploration

- **Morning:** Visit Belém. See Belém Tower and Jerónimos Monastery. Try Pastéis de Belém.
- **Afternoon:** Explore Parque das Nações, see the Oceanarium, and take a cable car ride.
- **Evening:** Dinner in Chiado or Bairro Alto with Fado music.

Day 3: Day Trip to Sintra

- **Morning:** Visit Pena Palace and Moorish Castle. Explore Quinta da Regaleira.
- **Afternoon:** Explore Sintra National Palace and meander through Sintra's historic town.
- **Evening:** Return to Lisbon. Dinner at Alfama or Baixa.

Day 4-5: Porto

Day 4: Travel to Porto

- **Morning:** Travel to Porto (approximately 3 hours by rail or automobile).
- **Afternoon:** Explore Porto's historic center, see Clérigos Tower and Lello Bookstore.

- **Evening:** Dinner at Ribeira overlooking the Douro River.

Day 5: Douro Valley

- **Morning:** Explore the Douro Valley. Visit a wine vineyard for sampling.
- **Afternoon:** Scenic drive along the Douro River. Visit vistas in communities like Pinhão.
- **Evening:** Return to Porto. Dinner with Porto wine.

Day 6-7: Coimbra and Aveiro

Day 6: Coimbra

- **Morning:** Travel to Coimbra (approximately 1 hour from Porto). Visit the University of Coimbra and Joanina Library.
- **Afternoon:** Explore Coimbra's historic center and botanical park.
- **Evening:** Return to Porto or stay overnight in Coimbra.

Day 7: Aveiro

- **Morning:** Travel to Aveiro (approximately 1 hour from Porto). Explore the canals by boat or moliceiro.
- **Afternoon:** Visit Costa Nova beach and beautiful striped buildings. Taste classic ovos moles.
- **Evening:** Return to Porto or stay overnight in Aveiro.

Day 8-10: Algarve

Day 8: Faro and Algarve

- **Morning:** Fly to Faro or drive to Algarve (approximately 3 hours from Lisbon or 2 hours from Porto).
- **Afternoon:** Explore Faro's historic town and see the Cathedral of Faro.
- **Evening:** Dinner overlooking the marina.

Day 9: Algarve Coastal Exploration

- **Morning:** Visit Ponta do Piedade and Cabo de São Vicente for natural beauty.
- **Afternoon:** Relax on beaches like Praia da Marinha or Praia da Rocha.
- **Evening:** Dinner in Lagos or Portimão.

Day 10: Algarve Historical Towns

- **Morning:** Visit ancient places like Lagos or Silves with Moorish architecture.
- **Afternoon:** Explore local markets and taste local food.
- **Evening:** Return to Faro or drive back to Lisbon/Porto for departure.

Tips for Your Trip:

- **Transportation:** Rent a vehicle for flexibility, particularly for touring the Douro Valley and Algarve. Use trains for lengthier travels between cities.
- **Tickets:** Book tickets in advance for famous destinations like Pena Palace, wine tastings in Douro Valley, and flights to/from Faro.
- **Local Cuisine:** Sample regional delicacies throughout your vacation, including bacalhau meals, pastéis de nata, and seafood in the Algarve.

This itinerary offers a complete tour of Portugal's main cities, cultural sites, natural landscapes, and seaside beauty, ensuring you experience the most of what this unique nation has to offer over 10 days.

Printed in Great Britain
by Amazon